Level 5

Caribbean Primary

Mathematics

6th edition

Contributors

Jonella Giffard
Hyacinth Dorleon
Melka Daniel
Martiniana Smith
Troy Nestor
Lydon Richardson
Rachel Mason
Eugenia Charles
Sharon Henry-Phillip
Glenroy Phillip
Jeffrey Blaize
Clyde Fitzpatrick
Reynold Francis
Wilma Alexander
Rodney Julien
C. Ellsworth Diamond
Shara Quinn

HODDER
EDUCATION
AN HACHETTE UK COMPANY

Contents

Contents

How to use this book

This Student's Book meets the objectives of the OECS and regional curricula for Level 5. The Student's Book provides both learning notes marked as Explain and a wide range of activities to help and encourage students to meet the learning outcomes for the level.

The content is arranged in topics, which correspond to the strands in the syllabus. For example, Topics 2, 5 and 9 relate to the strand of Number sense, while Topics 4 and 12 relate to the various aspects that need to be covered in the strand of Geometry (Shape and space).

Topic 1, **Getting ready** is a revision topic that allows you to do a baseline assessment of key skills and concepts covered in the previous level. You may need to revise some of these concepts if students are uncertain or struggle with them.

Each topic begins with an opening spread with the following features:

Notes for teachers about key mathematical skills that need to be developed.

Questions to discuss with the students as they begin a new topic.

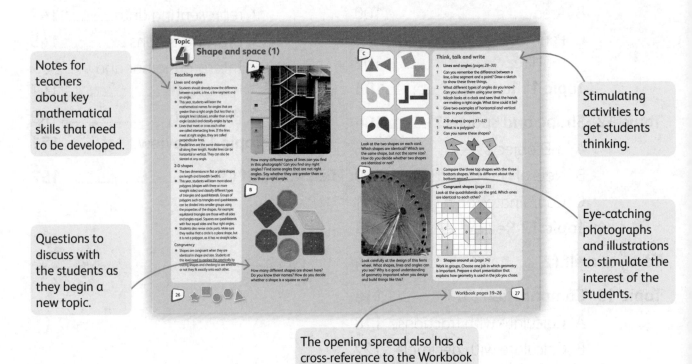

Stimulating activities to get students thinking.

Eye-catching photographs and illustrations to stimulate the interest of the students.

The opening spread also has a cross-reference to the Workbook pages that support the topic.

The questions and photographs relate to the specific sections of each topic. You can let the students do all the activities (A, B and C, for example) as you start a topic, or you can do only the activities that relate to the section you are about to start.

Topics 2–15 are subdivided into units that deal with different skills that need to be developed to meet the learning outcomes. For example, Topic 2, **Number sense (1)** is divided into three units: **A** Counting and place value, **B** Compare and order numbers and **C** Rounding and estimating.

Each unit is structured in a similar way.

A student-friendly list of learning objectives.

A key word list – the words are bold and blue in the text.

Graded activities for consolidation.

Teaching text that explains concepts and provides examples.

Problem-solving activities.

Challenge activities to stretch students' abilities.

Discussion questions to make connections to prior learning.

A review activity.

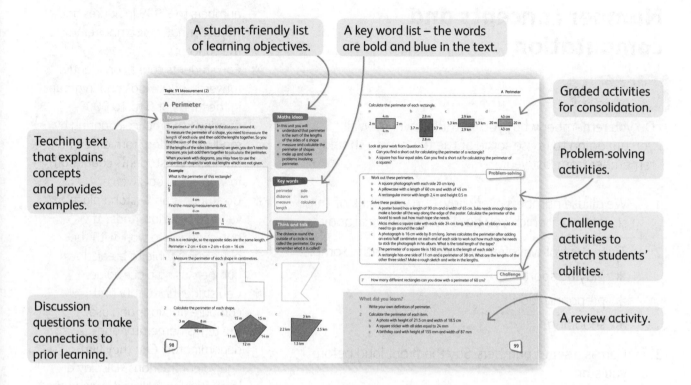

As you work through the units you will find a range of different types of activities and tasks, including practical investigations, problem-solving strategies, projects and challenge activities. These features are clearly marked in the book so you know what you are dealing with.

The topics end with a review section that provides:
* *An interactive summary* activity to help students consolidate and reflect on what they've learnt.
* *Think, talk, write* … activities that encourage students to share ideas, clarify their thinking and write in their maths journals.
* *A quick check* revision exercise which includes questions from all the units.

There are three tests provided in the Student's Book to allow for ongoing assessment and to prepare students for formal testing at all levels. Test 1 covers work from Topics 1–6, Test 2 covers work from Topics 1–12 and Test 3 covers work from the entire book.

Topic 1

Getting ready

Number concepts and computation

Explain

Do you remember what you learnt in Level 4? Well, you are going to revise some of the things you should remember from last year.

1 We all use numbers every day. Can you think of three situations in which you have used numbers today?

2 Try to think of ways fractions are used in each example:
   * playing sport
   * preparing food
   * shopping.

3 Here is a set of numbers. Say them out loud before you start.

| 345 | 1 098 | 9 089 | $\frac{5}{9}$ | 2 006 |

   a List the whole numbers in descending order.
   b What type of numbers are the others?
   c Write two fractions that are equivalent to $\frac{5}{9}$.
   d Which number has 9 in the tens place?
   e Which two whole numbers are odd numbers? How do you know this?
   f Write a new number between 2 500 and 2 600. It should be an even number with a 7 in the tens place and a digit < 6 in the ones place.
   g What is the value of each digit in the number 9 089?

4 Write each number in expanded notation.
   a 876   b 2 346

5 Work out the patterns. Write the next three numbers in each sequence.
   a 1, 8, 15, 22, …
   b 89, 83, 77, 71, …
   c 448, 224, 112, …

6   Find the highest common factor (HCF) of each set of numbers.

    a   15 and 20   b   12 and 16

    c   12, 16 and 20

7   Find the lowest common multiple (LCM) of each set of numbers.

    a   2 and 3   b   4 and 5

    c   2, 4 and 5

8   Calculate mentally. Write the answers only.

    a   27 + 33   b   90 × 6

    c   double 120   d   19 + 230

    e   250 + 10   f   400 ÷ 2

9   Do these calculations. Show how you work each one out.

    a   234 + 567   b   2 347 + 5 009

    c   1 299 − 554   d   3 203 − 1 416

    e   234 × 5   f   264 ÷ 3

10   Estimate by rounding and then calculate the answers.

    a   2 341 + 1 408   b   1 987 − 1 235

    c   2 000 − 1 209

11   Calculate.

    a $\frac{1}{6} + \frac{3}{6}$ b $\frac{4}{7} + \frac{2}{7} - \frac{3}{7}$ c $\frac{1}{4} + \frac{7}{16}$

12   Say whether each number sentence is true or false. If it is false, write a correction.

    a   1 345 + 1 > 1 356   b   9 800 ÷ 9 800 = 0   c   3 002 + 202 < 5 022

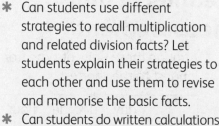

* Can students use different strategies to recall multiplication and related division facts? Let students explain their strategies to each other and use them to revise and memorise the basic facts.
* Can students do written calculations in all four operations with larger numbers? Let them check each other's work and observe them as they do calculations to correct any misconceptions or mistakes. Allow the use of different methods and strategies.
* Can students add and subtract fractions with different but related denominators? Can they multiply fractions by whole numbers? Continue to use concrete models and diagrams to demonstrate and model this.

Problem-solving

13   A diamond ring costs $1 470.00 and a ruby ring costs $968.00.

    a   Estimate and then work out the total cost of the two rings.

    b   How much cheaper is the ruby ring than the diamond ring?

    c   The shop sells three ruby rings. How much money does it receive?

    d   Martin and James buy the ruby ring for their mom. They split the cost equally. How much do they each pay?

14   Kaylee did the following workings to solve a word problem. Write a possible problem for these workings.

$$3 \times 15 = (3 \times 10) + (3 \times 5)$$
$$= 30 + 15$$
$$= 45$$

$$\begin{array}{r} 1\overset{4}{\cancel{5}}\overset{1}{0} \\ -\ 45 \\ \hline 105 \end{array}$$

Geometry and measurement

1   Arrange these units of time from the longest to the shortest.

| day   decade   hour |
| leap year   minute   month |
| second   week   year |

2   What do you call a 2-D shape with four equal sides and four right angles?

3   Choose the most accurate temperature in each case.

   a   Your normal body temperature:
       12 °C   36 °C   56 °C

   b   Cold water taken from a fridge:
       3 °C   28 °C   43 °C

   c   Boiling water in a kettle:
       56 °C   98 °C   180 °C

4   a   Draw a rectangle with sides of 3 cm and 6 cm.

   b   Calculate the perimeter of the rectangle.

5   A rectangle has a perimeter of 24 centimetres. The length is double the width. What is the width of the rectangle?

6   These clocks all show a.m. times. Write the times in order from earliest to latest.

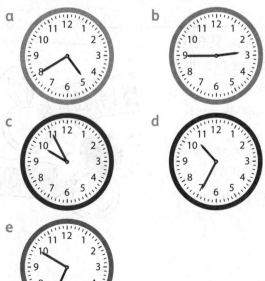

Teaching notes

Check:

✳   Can students name and group 2-D shapes and 3-D objects using shape properties? Remind students to count sides and compare the lengths of sides and the sizes of angles. Ask questions such as: How many shapes can you see with four sides? Which of these sides are all the same length? Which shapes have only three sides? How many faces does this solid have? What shape are the faces?

✳   Can students recognise and name line segments and right angles? Revise the terms as necessary and let the students make a folded corner of a page to measure angles to see if they are greater or smaller than a right angle.

✳   Are students able to say whether a shape is symmetrical or not and to identify and draw lines of symmetry on diagrams? Encourage students to trace and fold shapes to decide whether they are symmetrical if they struggle to do this visually.

✳   Do students understand the concept of perimeter and can they measure and calculate perimeter? Make sure students know they need to add the lengths of all sides of a shape and that if lengths are given in a diagram they should not measure.

✳   Can students tell time up to one-minute intervals? Display a clock in the classroom or have a smaller clock for each group. Stop during the day at appropriate times to let them work out what time it is.

✳   Are students able to work with different units of time and to state the relationship between these? Let students make up and solve simple problems involving units of time. For example, how many weeks in two years? Use a clock and calendar regularly to revise and reinforce the relationships between units (days, weeks and months; fractions of an hour, and so on).

✳   Can students describe the money they use? Let them use real coins and notes, or provide pictures to reinforce money concepts. Let students play games involving counting money, paying amounts and making up amounts in different ways so that students become familiar with money and its value.

Statistics

1 Use the data in the picture.

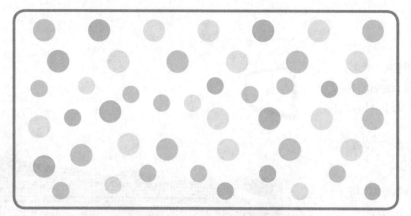

a Copy this table and use tallies to complete it.

Characteristics of ball	Yellow	Blue	Green
Large			
Small			

b Draw a pictograph to show how many small balls there are of each colour.

c Draw a bar graph to show how many larger balls there are of each colour.

2 Aaliyah is selling lemonade in her neighbourhood after school for some extra pocket money. She made a graph of her sales for the week.

a What is the title of this graph?
b On which day did Aaliyah sell the most lemonade?
c On which day did she sell 45 glasses of lemonade?
d How many glasses did she sell on Tuesday?

Topic 2 Number sense (1)

Teaching notes

Count in a higher number range

* Students should be able to use the patterns they already know to count beyond 9 999 (up to at least 100 000).
* It is important to continue to provide regular and ongoing opportunities for counting.

Understand place value to thousands

* For numbers above 9 999, the place value table is extended to the left to include a place for ten thousands.
* Numbers can be written as a sum of the values in each place. This is called expanded notation. For example: 26 345 = 20 000 + 6 000 + 300 + 40 + 5
* The position (place) of a digit affects its value. In the number 26 345, the digit 3 has a value of 300 because it is in the hundreds place. The 2 has a value of 20 000 because it is in the ten thousands place.

Rounding and estimating

* The rules for rounding off numbers apply to all places. Students should be familiar with this concept and they should understand how to use the digit to the right of the rounding place to decide how to round the number. If that digit is 5 or greater, you add 1 to the rounding place digit, if it is 4 or less you leave it as is. Then you fill in 0 in the places to the right of the rounding digit.
* Estimating involves doing a rough calculation (normally with rounded values) to check whether an answer is reasonable or not. You can round to the number of places in the smallest value, or to the first digit (from the left) in each figure. This is called leading figure rounding.

Compare and order numbers

* Comparing numbers involves deciding whether a number is greater than (>) or less than (<) another number.
* Ordering numbers means putting a set into ascending or descending order.
* Place value is important for comparing and ordering numbers.

A large cruise ship can carry nearly eight thousand passengers and crew. It has over two thousand six hundred guest rooms. Can you write these numbers? What is the biggest number you can write and say?

This is part of the crowd at a large international football match between Cameroon and the Netherlands. Estimate how many people there are. Tell your partner how you found this figure.

Think, talk and write

A Counting and place value (pages 8–10)

There were 6 156 passengers on a cruise.

1 Write the number of passengers in words.
2 What is the value of the 5 in the number?
3 What digit is in the ones place?
4 What number is 100 more than 6 156?

Now use the four digits from 6 156.

5 What is the greatest number you can make?
6 What is the smallest number you can make?
7 What is the difference between the greatest and smallest number you made?

B Compare and order numbers (pages 11–12)

Read the information on the diagram.

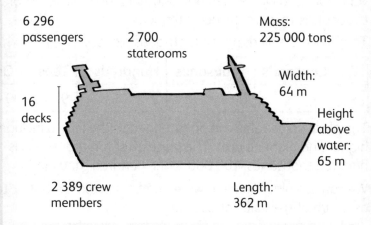

6 296 passengers   2 700 staterooms   Mass: 225 000 tons

16 decks   Width: 64 m

Height above water: 65 m

2 389 crew members   Length: 362 m

1 Divide the numbers into two groups. One group should have numbers that are smaller than 9 999 and the other should have numbers that are greater than 9 999.
2 Explain how you decided whether each number was greater than 9 999 or not.

C Rounding and estimating (pages 13–14)

Nina says, 'There are about 400 children in my school'.

1 Does this mean there are exactly 400 children in the school? Explain why or why not.
2 If we assume that Nina rounded the number correctly, could there be 350 children in the school? Why?
3 Could there be 450 children in the school? Why?

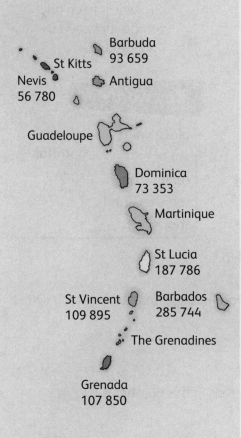

Barbuda 93 659
St Kitts
Nevis 56 780   Antigua
Guadeloupe
Dominica 73 353
Martinique
St Lucia 187 786
St Vincent 109 895   Barbados 285 744
The Grenadines
Grenada 107 850

This map shows the population of seven countries in the Eastern Caribbean in 2017. Which country had the greatest population? Which country had the smallest population? What is the rank of your country?

A Counting and place value

Maths ideas

In this unit you will:
* extend the place value table to include ten thousands, thousands, hundreds, tens and units
* state the place value and total value of any digit in numbers up to 100 000
* use expanded notation to write numbers
* count forwards and backwards from any number between 0 and 100 000.

Explain

You already know that we use **place value** to help us read and write large numbers.

The **value** of any **digit** in a number depends on its place in the number.

The value of each digit in the numbers 9 999 and 1 000 is shown below.

Thousands	Hundreds	Tens	Ones
9	9	9	9
1	0	0	0

If we add these two numbers, we get a number with **ten thousands**.

You cannot have more than 9 in any column in the place value table, so we need to add another place to the left of the **thousands** to write the new number.

That place is called the ten thousands place.

Ten thousands	Thousands	Hundreds	Tens	Ones
1	0	9	9	9

The place value table can be extended to the left to include higher and higher places. The place after ten thousands is called hundred thousands. 100 000 is one hundred thousand.

We can use place value to write numbers in **expanded notation**. To **expand** a number you write it as a sum of the value of each digit.

4 639 = 4 000 + 600 + 30 + 9

21 506 = 20 000 + 1 000 + 500 + 6

The 0 in the tens place is a place holder. It shows there are no tens in this number.

Key words

place value
value
digit
ten thousands
thousands
expanded notation
expand

1   Read the number names. Write each number in numerals.
   a   four thousand seven hundred and twenty-three
   b   twelve thousand three hundred and nine
   c   twenty-five thousand four hundred and seventy-four
   d   one hundred and sixty-three thousand four hundred and twelve
   e   three hundred and seven thousand two hundred and eighty-nine
   f   nine hundred and ninety-nine thousand nine hundred and ninety-nine

2   Express each number in words.
   a   3 507   b   12 089   c   30 689   d   95 125

3 Write each sum as an ordinary number.

    a 5 000 + 300 + 30 + 8

    b 50 000 + 8 000 + 900 + 40 + 3

    c 90 000 + 3 000 + 600 + 70 + 1

    d 80 000 + 3 000 + 800 + 90 + 3

    e 90 000 + 4 000 + 700 + 20 + 5

    f 80 000 + 9 000 + 600 + 30 + 9

4 What is the value of the red five in each number?

    a 23 5**0**8   **b** **5**4 000   **c** 1**5** 876

    d **5**1 500   **e** 34 09**5**   **f** 49 0**5**0

5 Write the number that is:

    a 100 more than 3 456   **b** 4 000 greater than 12 000

    c 10 less than 6 875   **d** 1 more than 23 459

    e 1 000 less than 24 560   **f** 10 more than 21 690

Problem-solving

6 Look at the flow diagram for sorting five-digit numbers.

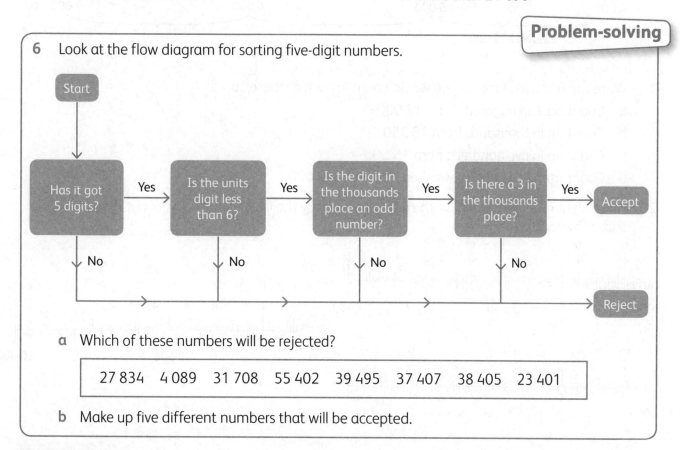

    a Which of these numbers will be rejected?

        | 27 834   4 089   31 708   55 402   39 495   37 407   38 405   23 401 |

    b Make up five different numbers that will be accepted.

Investigate

7 Write these four digits on separate pieces of paper: 6   3   8   4

    a How many four-digit numbers can you make with more than five in the thousands place?

    b How many four-digit numbers can you make with an odd number of hundreds?

Counting on and counting back

When you count, you need to think about the direction in which you are counting. Counting on means the numbers get bigger in value. Counting back means the numbers get smaller in value.

When you skip count, the numbers increase or decrease in intervals.

> For example: 500, 550, 600, 650, … – these numbers are increasing in intervals of 50.
>
> 32 000, 31 000, 30 000, 29 000, … – these numbers are decreasing in intervals of 1 000.

When you use number lines to show larger numbers, you cannot show all the numbers. The little marks on the number line are placed at intervals.

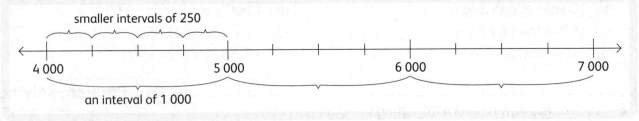

1   Write the first five numbers you would count in each of these cases.

   a   Count back in hundreds from 12 000

   b   Count on in thousands from 18 350

   c   Count up in five hundreds from 15 500

   d   Count from 16 250 backwards in intervals of 2 000

2   For each number line, work out the interval shown by the lines and then work out the number shown by each arrow.

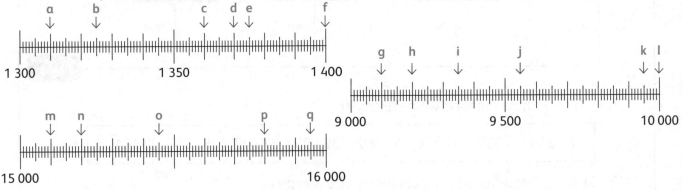

What did you learn?

Write these numbers in numerals and in words.

1   A five-digit number that is also an odd number.

2   A five-digit number that has 0 in the ones and in the thousands positions.

3   The amount that is 1 015 more than 10 000.

4   The number that is 10 000 more than 77 544.

B Compare and order numbers

Maths ideas

In this unit you will:
* use place value to compare and order large numbers.

Explain

We **compare** numbers to see which number is **greater than** or **less than** another number.

Place value is very useful for comparing numbers.

Read through the examples as a reminder of how to do this.

> **Example**
>
> Which number is greater in each pair?
>
>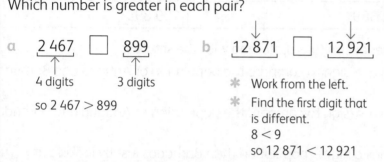
>
> a   2 467 ☐ 899
>
> 4 digits   3 digits
>
> so 2 467 > 899
>
> b   12 871 ☐ 12 921
>
> * Work from the left.
> * Find the first digit that is different.
>
> 8 < 9
>
> so 12 871 < 12 921

Key words

compare	order
greater than	ascending
less than	descending

You can also arrange sets of numbers in **order** of size. Numbers that go up in value are in **ascending** order. Numbers that go down in value are in **descending** order.

Any whole number with more digits will always be greater than a number with fewer digits:

1 000 > 999 and 6 543 < 10 000

When numbers have the same number of digits, you can use place value to sort them. It is useful to do this in steps to avoid mistakes.

> **Example**
>
> Arrange these numbers in descending order:
>
> 1 482, 2 487, 1 918, 2 562
>
> 1 482   2 487   1 918   2 562   All have four digits, so sort using thousands first.
>   2 thousand > 1 thousand
>
> 2 487   2 562   1 482   1 918
>   5 is greater   9 is greater   Look at the hundreds next.
>
> Write the numbers in descending order:
>
> 2 562, 2 487, 1 918, 1 482

1   Write each set of numbers in ascending order.

    a   9 287, 9 812, 9 187, 9 712, 9 127

    b   14 141, 14 441, 14 414, 14 114

    c   81 188, 88 881, 88 818, 81 818

    d   43 219, 78 106, 45 000, 71 992

2   Read the information in the table.

Country	Area (square kilometres)	Population (2017)
Antigua and Barbuda	442	93 659
Barbados	430	73 353
Dominica	751	285 744
Grenada	344	107 850
St Kitts and Nevis	261	56 780
St Lucia	617	187 768
St Vincent and the Grenadines	389	109 895

a   Write the country names in order of size (area), starting with the smallest.

b   Write a number statement with a > sign to compare the population of Antigua and Barbuda and Barbados.

c   Write a number statement with a < sign to compare the population of Antigua and Barbuda and St Kitts and Nevis.

d   How can you tell that St Lucia has a higher population than Barbados just by looking at the figures?

Problem-solving

3   For each card, make the largest and smallest possible number using all the digits.

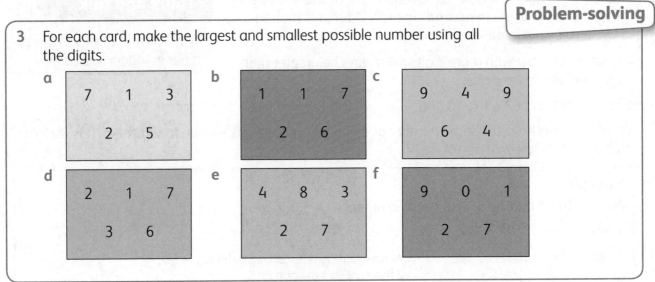

a

7   1   3

2   5

b

1   1   7

2   6

c

9   4   9

6   4

d

2   1   7

3   6

e

4   8   3

2   7

f

9   0   1

2   7

What did you learn?

Use the numbers from Question 3.

1   Arrange the set of greatest numbers in ascending order.

2   Arrange the set of smallest numbers in descending order.

C Rounding and estimating

Explain

We use **place value** to **round off** numbers.
* Find the **digit** in the rounding place.
* Look at the digit to the right of this place.
  * If the digit to the right is 0, 1, 2, 3 or 4, leave the digit in the rounding place as it is.
  * If the digit to the right is 5, 6, 7, 8 or 9, add 1 to the digit in the rounding place.
* Change all the digits to the right of the rounding place to 0.

Example 1

Round off 43 269 to the **nearest** thousand.

This is the thousands place.

T H T O
4 3 2 6 9   This is the digit to the right. It is 2, so leave the 3 in the thousands as it is.

4 3 0 0 0

Write zeros in all the places to the right.

Example 2

Round 18 763 to the nearest hundred.

This is the hundreds place.

T H T O
1 8 7 6 3   This digit is more than 5, so we change the 7 in the hundreds to 8.

1 8 8 0 0

Write zeros in all the places to the right.

Estimation is a very useful strategy to help you calculate quickly and to help you decide whether your answer is reasonable or not. You can use rounding to **estimate** an approximate answer.

For most estimated answers you can use leading figure rounding.

This means that you round each number to the digit in the highest place (the first one from the left).

Example 3

Estimate 468×62

500×60 Round off each number to the first digit.

$5 \times 6 = 30$ Use the facts you already know.

So $500 \times 60 = 30\,000$

$468 \times 62 \approx 30\,000$ $\approx$ means 'approximately equal to'

When you give an estimated answer, you use the $\approx$ symbol.

Example 4

Estimate $416 + 338 + 147 + 407$

$\begin{array}{r} 400 \\ 300 \\ 100 \\ + 400 \\ \hline 1\,200 \end{array}$ Round off each number to the first digit.

So $416 + 338 + 147 + 407 \approx 1\,200$

Maths ideas

In this unit you will:
* revise the rules for rounding numbers
* round numbers to the nearest ten, hundred and thousand
* use rounded numbers to estimate answers to calculations.

Key words

place value
round off
digit
nearest
estimate

Important symbol

$\approx$ approximately equal to

1   Round each number to the nearest hundred.
    a   1 645   b   5 570   c   3 470   d   19 876   e   12 499

2   Round each number to the nearest ten.
    a   1 088   b   66   c   12 603   d   3 721   e   199

3   Round each number to the nearest thousand.
    a   23 987   b   97 302   c   13 876   d   76 540   e   12 045

4   List all the numbers in the box that will give 6 000 when they are rounded to the nearest thousand.

    | 5 098 | 5 890 | 5 499 | 6 023 | 6 500 | 5 500 | 7 023 | 6 499 |

5   Say whether each statement is true or false.
    a   8 731 rounds to 9 000   b   12 800 rounds to 13 000
    c   12 458 rounds to 12 500   d   28 107 rounds to 28 110

6   Use rounding to estimate the answer to each calculation.
    a   39 + 42   b   499 − 67   c   32 876 − 12 909   d   29 + 187
    e   148 − 9 + 24   f   363 + 98   g   234 + 123 + 97   h   32 × 12
    i   1 823 − 1 015   j   2 876 + 3 087   k   58 × 22   l   2 344 ÷ 9

Problem-solving

7   Use the scale on the diagram to estimate the distance from:
    a   Townsville to the Harbour
    b   Beachville to Cityville by road
    c   Farmville to Beachville and back, three times a week.

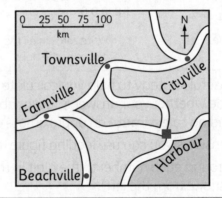

8   Crowd attendance at a cricket match over a three-day period was 4 146, 5 964 and 7 193.
    a   Estimate the total attendance.
    b   If tickets cost $9 per day, estimate how much money was spent on tickets over the three days.

What did you learn?

1   Round each number to the nearest thousand.
    a   12 345   b   9 806   c   980   d   34 764

2   Is the number 38 830 closer to 39 000 or to 38 500? Which figure would you use to give the approximate population of a town? Why?

Topic 2 Review

Key ideas and concepts

Read the statements. Fill in the missing words to summarise what you learnt in this topic.

1 A number in the _____ has five digits.

2 Each _____ in a number has its own place value.

3 Writing a number as _____ is called expanded notation.

4 Ascending order means the numbers _____ in value.

5 To round a number to the nearest _____, you look at the digit in the hundreds place.

6 When you round numbers in a calculation, you get an _____ answer.

Think, talk, write …

1 Explain in your own words how to:
   a say the number 36 016
   b compare the numbers 56 089 and 56 908.

2 Give three examples of where you might use or hear large rounded numbers in everyday life.

Quick check

1 Write the number you would get if you:
   a added 5 hundreds to 14 499
   b added a thousand to 24 000
   c added 1 to 79 999.

2 What is the value of the red digit in each of these numbers?
   a 23 45**7**   b **6**5 432   c **7**6 309   d 30 7**6**5

3 Here is a set of numbers.
   23 456   32 906   76 400   23 509
   a Write each number in expanded notation.
   b Compare the 1st and 4th numbers using a $<$ sign.
   c Rewrite the numbers in ascending order.
   d Which number will be 23 500 when rounded to the nearest hundred?

4 Use rounding to estimate the answers to these calculations.
   a 603 + 715 + 986   b 7 899 − 5 211   c 999 ÷ 2   d 408 × 31

5 Round the side lengths to the nearest ten and estimate the perimeter of each shape.

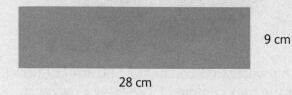

9 cm

28 cm

19 cm

21 cm

Teaching notes

Mental strategies

✱ Continue to start each lesson with a short mental activity whenever possible to give students a chance to use number facts and consolidate strategies (such as partitioning, compensating or bridging through multiples of 10). Students only develop fluency and confidence if you provide regular and ongoing practice.

✱ Encourage mathematical thinking and reasoning. This involves making time to talk about how students worked out their answers. Let students show their working on the board and let them verbalise and explain the steps they took. Others will learn from these explanations, as they become exposed to different options and methods. This allows them to consider multiple strategies and choose the one they find easiest and most efficient.

Pen-and-paper calculations in a higher number range

✱ Students will perform addition and subtraction that involves an exchange (regrouping) across place values. Treat this as a normal element of calculating rather than as something difficult.

✱ Allow students to model calculations using place value and number lines until they are comfortable using the more formal column methods.

✱ Remember that the word 'sum' only applies to addition, so avoid using it to talk about other operations.

Problem-solving strategies

✱ Students need to realise that some problems are multi-step. In these problems they need to first calculate one value that they can use in the next step.

✱ Model the steps and talk students through your method of working. This makes problem-solving strategies visible to students who have not yet fully understood them.

A

Think about buying items at a shop. What mental arithmetic do people do when they are shopping? Share your ideas with your group.

C

This water tank can hold 2 500 litres of water. If the tank contains 1 728 litres, how much more water is needed to fill it? Show how you worked this out.

1234

B

When you play darts, you get points depending on where the dart lands. The bull's-eye in the middle is worth 50. What is the total score of these darts? Show how you worked out the answer.

D

The smaller cruise ship carries 2 744 passengers and has 833 crew members. The larger ship carries 5 412 passengers and has 2 394 crew members. How would you work out the total number of passengers both ships carry? How would you work out how many more crew the larger ship needs? How would you estimate the difference in passenger numbers?

Think, talk and write

A **Mental strategies** (pages 18–19)

Calculate mentally.

1   57 + 40
2   34 + 25
3   730 + 140
4   65 – 30
5   85 – 23
6   430 – 120

B **Addition** (pages 20–21)

On one weekend, 4 654 cruise passengers visited an island on Saturday and 3 875 visited on Sunday. Estimate the total number of cruise passengers for the weekend. Tell your partner how you got your answer. Then calculate the actual total.

C **Subtraction** (pages 22–23)

A cruise ship carrying 5 409 passengers docked in St John's and 4 023 passengers left the ship. How many remained on board? Tell your partner how you worked out your answer.

D **Mixed problems with addition and subtraction** (page 24)

Use the information about the two cruise ships for this activity.

1   Make up two problems of your own using the information and solve them.
2   Use a calculator to check your solutions.
3   Exchange problems with a partner and solve each other's problems.
4   Check your partner's solution and explain where he or she went wrong if they made any mistakes.

A Mentalstrategies

Explain

Do you remember these **mental strategies** for adding and subtracting quickly?

Use the **pattern** of facts you already know. You know that:

13 + 6 = 19

so 130 + 60 = 190 and 1 300 + 600 = 1 900.

You can also **break down** numbers and use **place value**.

Jottings can help you keep track in this strategy.

64 + 27

80 + 11 → 91

64 – 27
64 – 20 – 4 – 3
44 – 4 – 3
40 – 3 = 37

You can **compensate** so that you can work with easier numbers. Compensation is useful when adding or subtracting 8, 9, 11 or 12.

To add 8, add 10, then subtract 2 from the answer.	14 + 8 = 24 – 2 = 22
To add 9, add 10, then subtract 1 from the answer.	14 + 9 = 24 – 1 = 23
To add 11, add 10, then another 1.	14 + 11 = 24 + 1 = 25
To add 12, add 10, then another 2.	14 + 12 = 24 + 2 = 26
To subtract 8, subtract 10, then add back 2.	54 – 8 = 44 + 2 = 46
To subtract 9, subtract 10, then add back 1.	54 – 9 = 44 + 1 = 45
To subtract 11, subtract 10, then subtract another 1.	80 – 11 = 70 – 1 = 69
To subtract 12, subtract 10, then subtract another 2.	80 – 12 = 70 – 2 = 68

Jump in chunks on your own **number line**.

Jump in chunks that make sense to you.

To add, jump on in chunks, starting from the greater number.

287 + 329 = ☐

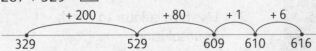

To subtract, jump back in chunks from the greater number.

483 – 219 = ☐

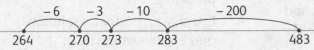

You can use any strategy when you calculate and you can combine strategies. Choose the strategy that works best for each calculation.

Maths ideas

In this unit you will:
* revise mental strategies for adding and subtracting
* practice using different strategies to see which numbers work for each method.

Key words

mental strategy	jottings
pattern	compensate
break down	jump
place value	number line

1   Add mentally. Use the strategy you find most useful.
    a   127 + 8   b   137 + 9   c   149 + 12   d   729 + 11
    e   247 + 30   f   157 + 30   g   268 + 20   h   248 + 110
    i   240 + 37   j   250 + 34   k   172 + 26   l   281 + 37
    m   430 + 210   n   814 + 180   o   245 + 126   p   338 + 122
    q   253 + 418   r   436 + 325   s   277 + 135   t   329 + 134

2   Subtract mentally. Use the strategy you find most useful.
    a   87 – 10   b   85 – 9   c   94 – 41   d   98 – 15
    e   85 – 14   f   96 – 9   g   88 – 37   h   95 – 22
    i   45 – 28   j   83 – 47   k   72 – 45   l   83 – 36
    m   128 – 113   n   216 – 84   o   312 – 129   p   847 – 325
    q   800 – 588   r   721 – 129   s   814 – 326   t   900 – 327

3   The map shows the distances (in kilometres) between places. Try to solve these problems mentally. Use jottings if you need to.

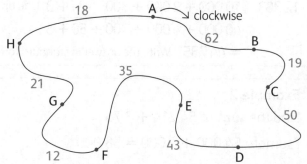

    a   What is the distance (clockwise) from:
        i   A to D?   ii   B to F?
        iii   C to G?   iv   A to G?
    b   James travels clockwise from A to F and back. How far does he travel in total?
    c   Nick wants to travels from H to D. He is not sure whether to drive clockwise or anti-clockwise. Which route is shorter? How much shorter is it?
    d   How much further is it from A to D if you travel clockwise instead of anti-clockwise?
    e   What is the total route distance?

4   The mass of nine items is given in kilograms. Mr Griffiths put three items on his truck. Their total mass was 90 kilograms. How many possible combinations of three different masses can you find to make 90 kilograms?

44 kg   40 kg   52 kg   18 kg   28 kg

6 kg   20 kg   30 kg   32 kg

What did you learn?

1   Calculate.
    a   33 + 19   b   832 – 29   c   412 + 578   d   1 764 – 1 213
    e   1 200 + 3 100   f   4 800 – 900   g   9 320 – 9 145   h   4 582 – 1 349

2   Tell your partner what strategy you used to find each answer. Explain why you chose that method of working.

B Addition

Explain

You have already done **addition** of numbers with up to four digits using **expanded notation** and the **column method**. The examples show you how to use each method to **add** numbers with five digits.

In this unit you will:

* use different methods to add numbers with up to four digits
* understand how to regroup numbers in any place
* use rounded numbers to find approximate answers (estimates)
* use estimates to decide whether an answer is reasonable or not.

Example 1

Add 32 452 + 12 303

Estimate 32 000 + 12 000 = 44 000

32 452	30 000 + 2 000 + 400 + 50 + 2	Use expanded notation.
12 303	10 000 + 2 000 + 300 + 3	Line up the places.
	40 000 + 4 000 + 700 + 50 + 5	
	= 44 755	Write the answer in standard form.

Key words

addition
expanded notation
column method
add
estimate
sum
place value
total
regroup
rounding
reasonable

Example 2

Find the **sum** of 54 214 + 3 751

Estimate 54 000 + 4 000 = 58 000

$$\begin{array}{r} 54\ 214 \\ +\ 3\ 751 \\ \hline 57\ 965 \end{array}$$

Write the digits with the same **place value** below each other.
Add up the columns.

Example 3

What is the **total** of 9 769 + 1 489?

Estimate 10 000 + 1 000 = 11 000

$$\begin{array}{r} {}^{1\ 1\ 1}\ \\ 9\ 769 \\ +\ 1\ 489 \\ \hline 11\ 258 \end{array}$$

Write the digits with the same place value below each other.
Add up the columns.
Regroup as you need to. Carry the tens to the next place.
9 + 9 = 18. Write the 8 in the ones place and carry 1 to the tens place.
6 + 8 = 14, 14 + 1 (regroup) = 15. Write the 5 in the tens place and carry 1 to the hundreds place.
7 + 4 = 11, 11 + 1 (regroup) = 12. Write the 2 in the hundreds place and carry 1 to the thousands place.
9 + 1 = 10, 10 + 1 (regroup) = 11. There are no more digits to add, so write 11 in the thousands place in the answer line.

You can use the method that you find easiest as long as you show your working.

Always estimate by **rounding** off the numbers before you add. This helps you to check that your answer is **reasonable**.

1   Estimate by rounding. Then add.
    a   955 + 223   b   2 345 + 1 054
    c   6 330 + 1 234   d   11 321 + 33 107
    e   4 105 + 89 235   f   4 640 + 25 608
    g   11 160 + 9 725   h   4 281 + 1 110
    i   7 342 + 11 013   j   423 + 11 024
    k   29 300 + 8 489   l   562 + 87 417

2   Write in columns and add.
    a   12 + 60 + 13   b   123 + 23 + 4 000
    c   241 + 2 400 + 10 000   d   12 400 + 238 + 20 000
    e   32 + 400 + 32 000 + 12   f   50 + 500 + 50 200

3   Use the method you find easiest to add these numbers. Estimate before you start working.
    a   437 + 876   b   398 + 1 209
    c   5 427 + 2 686   d   12 987 + 4 567
    e   5 412 + 19 234   f   28 435 + 32 876
    g   18 796 + 54 321   h   23 987 + 12 450
    i   24 999 + 54 230   j   45 076 + 32 987

4   Estimate and then calculate the answer.
    a   What is the sum of 12 345 and 14 098?
    b   Add 29 452 to 35 806.
    c   Find the sum of 1 345, 12 304 and 13 098.
    d   What is the total of 45 678 and 10 121?
    e   What number is 13 454 greater than 13 454?

Problem-solving

5   The sum of three numbers is 34 641. At least two of the numbers have
    five digits. Write five possible addition sums that will give this total.

6   A rectangular piece of land 8 564 m wide and 9 950 m long is to be marked out for a housing
    development. What is the perimeter of the land to be used?

What did you learn?
Calculate.

1   426 + 6 543 + 18 000 + 405

2   13 243 + 68 681

3   4 309 + 19 + 32 456 + 5

4   33 793 + 26 134

C Subtraction

Explain

You can use the same methods that you used for addition to do **subtraction** of larger numbers. Read through the examples to remind yourself how to **subtract** with and without **regrouping**.

Example 1

What is 87 324 − 23 103?

Estimate: 90 000 − 20 000 = 70 000

87 324   80 000 + 7 000 + 300 + 20 + 4
23 103   20 000 + 3 000 + 100   + 3
             60 000 + 4 000 + 200 + 20 + 1   Subtract the values
             = 64 221   in each place.

Example 2

Subtract 12 345 from 95 865.

Estimate: 100 000 − 10 000 = 90 000

$$\begin{array}{r} 95\ 865 \\ -\ 12\ 345 \\ \hline 83\ 520 \end{array}$$

Example 3

What is 14 675 **minus** 12 399?

Estimate: 15 000 − 12 000 = 3 000

Subtract the ones, rename the 7 to get 6 tens and 10 ones.
15 − 9 = 6

$$\begin{array}{r} 5\ ^{1}6\ 1 \\ 14\ \cancel{6}7\ 5 \\ -\ 12\ 3\ 9\ 9 \\ \hline 2\ 2\ 7\ 6 \end{array}$$

Subtract the tens, rename the 6.
16 − 9 = 7

Maths ideas

In this unit you will:
* use different methods to subtract numbers with up to five digits
* understand how to regroup numbers in any place
* use rounded numbers to find approximate answers (estimates)
* use estimates to decide whether an answer is reasonable.

Key words

subtraction
subtract
regrouping
estimate
minus
difference

---

1 Estimate and then subtract to find the answer.

   a   689 − 325   b   827 − 304   c   999 − 888

   d   1 400 − 1 200   e   3 225 − 224   f   8 234 − 4 317

   g   24 245 − 19 321   h   33 098 − 20 450   i   42 512 − 24 755

   j   76 312 − 35 980   k   99 765 − 12 098   l   48 982 − 45 897

2   a   Decrease thirteen thousand by three thousand and three.

   b   101 is taken away from 1 010. What remains?

   c   Mount Everest is 8 848 m high. Mount Kilimanjaro is 5 892 m high. What is the **difference** in height?

3   The population of the largest cities in some Caribbean countries (in 2017) is given below.

Kingstown
24 518

Castries
65 656

St George's
33 559

St John's
22 634

Roseau
16 571

Basseterre
12 920

Bridgetown
98 511

a   List the names of the cities and their populations in descending order (largest population first).

b   How many more people live in Bridgetown than in Castries?

c   What is the difference in population between Castries and Kingstown?

d   The combined population of two of the cities is 41 089. If one of the cities is Roseau, which is the other?

e   How many more people would need to move to St John's for it to have the same population as Castries?

4   Work with a partner.

a   Make up four subtraction problems of your own using the city populations. Work out the answers on a separate sheet.

b   Exchange your problems with another pair and solve each other's problems.

c   Swap back and check each other's work.

What did you learn?

Work out the missing value in each of these number sentences.

1   86 581 – ☐ = 38 657

2   ☐ – 45 728 = 25 245

3   22 656 – ☐ = 11 754

4   98 580 – ☐ = 29 484

5   ☐ – 38 795 = 21 317

6   36 921 – ☐ = 19 945

D Mixed problems with addition and subtraction

Maths ideas

In this unit you will:
* use what you have learnt in this topic to solve problems using two operations
* apply suitable strategies to help you solve problems using more than one step.

Explain

You can use addition and subtraction to solve many different kinds of mathematical problems.

Sometimes you need to do more than one **operation** to solve a problem. Read through the example to see how two students solved the same problem in different ways. Both did two steps to get to the answer.

Key words

operation
total

Example

The **total** population of an island is 23 630. If there are 7 562 adult men and 7 542 adult women, how many children are there?

James

$$
\begin{array}{r}
1\ 1\ 5\ ^1 2\ 1 \\
2\ 3\ \cancel{6}\cancel{3}\ 0 \\
-\ \ \ 7\ 5\ 6\ 2 \\
\hline
1\ 6\ 0\ 6\ 8
\end{array}
$$
Subtract the men.

$$
\begin{array}{r}
5\ 1 \\
1\ \cancel{6}\ 0\ 6\ 8 \\
-\ \ \ 7\ 5\ 4\ 2 \\
\hline
8\ 5\ 2\ 6
\end{array}
$$
Subtract the women.

There are 8 526 children.

Amalie

$$
\begin{array}{r}
1\ 1 \\
7\ 5\ 6\ 2 \\
+\ \ 7\ 5\ 4\ 2 \\
\hline
1\ 5\ 1\ 0\ 4
\end{array}
$$
adults

$$
\begin{array}{r}
1\ 1\ \ \ \ 2\ 1 \\
2\ 3\ 6\ \cancel{3}\ 0 \\
-\ 1\ 5\ 1\ 0\ 4 \\
\hline
8\ 5\ 2\ 6
\end{array}
$$
children

There are 8 526 children.

1   What is 237 less than the sum of 13 453 and 8 765?

2   A car salesperson buys a car for $23 456.00 and then sells it for $25 000.00. How much money did he make on the sale?

3   A farmer had 13 753 banana trees on one plantation and 18 348 on another. During a hurricane, 2 367 trees were destroyed. How many were left?

4   At the beginning of a year, Mrs Smith had $26 732.00 in her savings account. At the end of the year, she had $28 617.00 in the account. How much more did she have at the end of the year?

5   The solutions to three different problems are given below. For each one, write a word problem that fits the number sentences.
   a   3 456 + 12 876 = 16 332
   b   763 + 987 = 1 750
       1 750 − 1 321 = 429
   c   28 + 147 + 305 = 480
       756 − 480 = 276

What did you learn?

A cruise ship leaves Fort Lauderdale with 2 309 passengers on board. It stops in Miami, where another 1 306 passengers board the ship. When it gets to Bridgetown, 298 passengers leave the cruise ship to fly home and another 407 board. How many passengers are on board for the return cruise?

Topic 3 Review

Key ideas and concepts

Copy the unit headings from this topic into your book. Write short notes to summarise the main things you learnt in each unit.

A Mental strategies

B Addition

C Subtraction

D Mixed problems with addition and subtraction

Think, talk, write ...

Work in pairs. Pretend you are teachers.

Make a poster for your class to teach them how to read and tackle word problems involving more than one step.

Use examples to help your students understand the work.

Quick check

1 Write each of these numbers in numerals.
   a three thousand four hundred and thirty-seven
   b twenty-one thousand eight hundred and twenty-nine
   c twelve thousand eight hundred and forty-seven
   d twenty-three thousand four hundred and two

2 Use the numbers in Question 1.
   a What is the sum of the numbers in parts **a** and **c**?
   b What is the total of all four numbers?
   c Find the difference between the sum of **a** and **b** and the sum of **c** and **d**.

3 Calculate.
   a 10 991 + 234 + 4 568
   b 32 819 + 43 214
   c 12 345 + 23 145
   d 11 285 – 9 873
   e 29 876 – 14 388
   f 64 000 – 39 453

4 Round to the nearest ten thousand to estimate the sum of 11 270, 22 701, 14 688 and 13 431. Calculate the difference between your estimate and the actual total.

5 The sum of three numbers is 12 345. Write four different addition sums that will give this result.

6 The difference between two five-digit numbers is 2 876. What could the numbers be?

Topic 4
Shape and space (1)

Teaching notes

Lines and angles

* Students should already know the difference between a point, a line, a line segment and an angle.
* This year, students will learn the mathematical names for angles that are greater than a right angle (but less than a straight line) (obtuse), smaller than a right angle (acute) and classify angles by type.
* Lines that meet or cross each other are called intersecting lines. If the lines meet at right angles, they are called perpendicular lines.
* Parallel lines are the same distance apart all along their length. Parallel lines can be horizontal or vertical. They can also be slanted at any angle.

2-D shapes

* The two dimensions in flat or plane shapes are length and breadth (width).
* This year, students will learn more about polygons (shapes with three or more straight sides) and classify different types of triangles and quadrilaterals. Groups of polygons such as triangles and quadrilaterals can be divided into smaller groups using the properties of the shapes. For example: equilateral triangles are those with all sides and angles equal. Squares are quadrilaterals with four equal sides and four right angles.
* Students also revise circle parts. Make sure they realise that a circle is a plane shape, but it is not a polygon, as it has no straight sides.

Congruency

* Shapes are congruent when they are identical in shape and size. Students at this level need to explore this practically by tracing shapes and checking to see whether or not they fit exactly onto each other.

A

How many different types of lines can you find in this photograph? Can you find any right angles? Find some angles that are not right angles. Say whether they are greater than or less than a right angle.

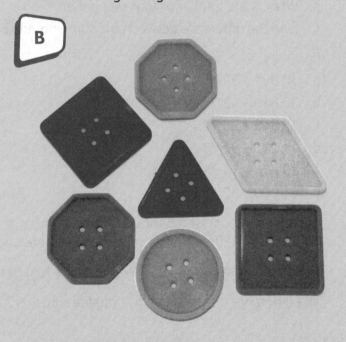

B

How many different shapes are shown here? Do you know their names? How do you decide whether a shape is a square or not?

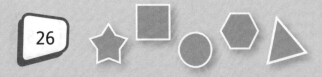

Look at the two shapes on each card. Which shapes are identical? Which are the same shape, but not the same size? How do you decide whether two shapes are identical or not?

Look carefully at the design of this ferris wheel. What shapes, lines and angles can you see? Why is a good understanding of geometry important when you design and build things like this?

Think, talk and write

A   Lines and angles *(pages 28–30)*

1   Can you remember the difference between a line, a line segment and a point? Draw a sketch to show these three things.

2   What different types of angles do you know? Can you show them using your arms?

3   Micah looks at a clock and sees that the hands are making a right angle. What time could it be?

4   Give two examples of horizontal and vertical lines in your classroom.

B   2-D shapes *(pages 31–32)*

1   What is a polygon?

2   Can you name these shapes?

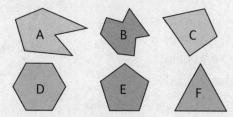

3   Compare the three top shapes with the three bottom shapes. What is different about the bottom group?

C   Congruent shapes *(page 33)*

Look at the quadrilaterals on the grid. Which ones are identical to each other?

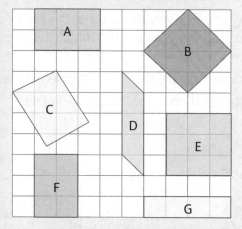

D   Shapes around us *(page 34)*

Work in groups. Choose one job in which geometry is important. Prepare a short presentation that explains how geometry is used in the job you chose.

A Lines and angles

Read through this information to make sure you remember what you learnt about **points**, **lines**, **line segments** and **angles** last year.

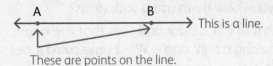

This is a line.

These are points on the line.

When lines meet or cross at a point they form an angle.

XY and ZY meet at Y to form this angle.

Y is a point. It is also the **vertex** of the angle.

Point Y is the vertex of the angle.

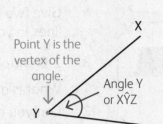

Angle Y or XŶZ

A line segment is part of a line. It has two end points.

Each side of this shape is a line segment.

There are four angles inside the shape.

Angle B is a **right angle**.

Angle A is greater than a right angle.

Angles C and D are both smaller than a right angle.

Angle A

Line segment AD

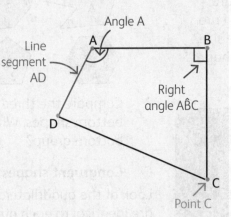

Right angle AB̂C

Point C

We can name angles using only the letter at the vertex or using three letters. If you use three letters, the middle letter must be the letter at the vertex.

Angles that are smaller than a right angle are called **acute angles**.

Angles that are greater than a right angle are called **obtuse angles**.

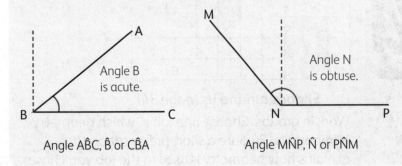

Angle B is acute.

Angle N is obtuse.

Angle AB̂C, B̂ or CB̂A   Angle MN̂P, N̂ or PN̂M

1 Draw and label:

    a line segment ST, 5 cm long

    b obtuse angle DÊF

    c right angle XŶZ, with acute angle VŶZ part of it.

2 Write the name of each angle marked on the diagram and state what type of angle it is (right, acute or obtuse).

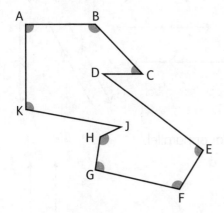

3   **a** Try to write all the digits from 0 to 9 so that each numeral only has straight line segments and right angles.

    b Try to write your name so that each letter contains only right angles.

4 Look at the triangles carefully.

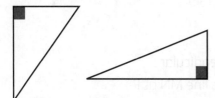 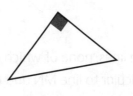 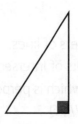

    a What type of angle is shaded red in each one?

    b What type of angle are the other two angles?

    c Is it possible for a triangle to have a right angle and an obtuse angle? Explain why or why not.

Explain

Lines can be drawn in any direction:

  * **horizontal** lines run across (east–west)

  * **vertical** lines run up and down (north–south)

  * **diagonal** lines run across from corner to corner.

Lines can cross each other. We say they **intersect** at a point.

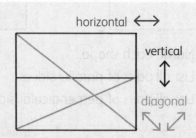

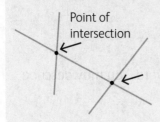

Point of intersection

When lines intersect or meet at right angles we say they are **perpendicular**.

The right-angle symbol shows that lines are perpendicular.

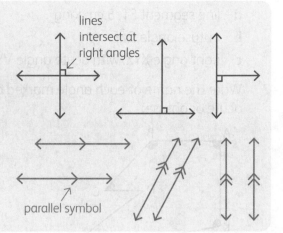

lines intersect at right angles

Parallel lines are lines that are the same distance apart all along their length. They run alongside each other and never meet or intersect.

The arrow symbols on the lines show they are parallel.

parallel symbol

5   Say whether each pair of lines is intersecting, perpendicular or parallel.

a   b   c   d   e

f   g   h   i   j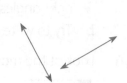

6   Draw these sets of lines.

   a   Three pairs of intersecting lines, none of which are perpendicular

   b   Line AB, which is perpendicular to line MN and intersects line MN at P

   c   Line MN // PQ

7   Look at these polygons.

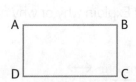   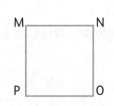   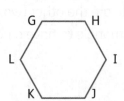

   a   Name each shape.

   b   List all pairs of parallel sides.

   c   List all pairs of perpendicular sides.

What did you learn?

1   Work with a partner. List the key words in this unit.

2   With your partner, try to find at least one real-life example for each key word. You may describe, draw or photograph the examples.

3   Share your ideas with the class.

B 2-D shapes

A plane shape is a two-dimensional figure. The two dimensions are length and width. Shapes with three or more straight sides are called **polygons**. Polygons are grouped and named according to the number of sides and angles the shape has. Some groups, such as **triangles** and **quadrilaterals**, contain different types of shapes.

The table shows the names and properties of some polygons.

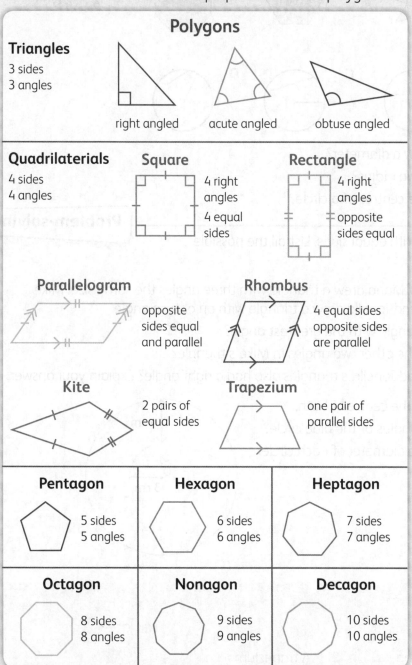

Polygons

Triangles
3 sides
3 angles

right angled   acute angled   obtuse angled

Quadrilaterials
4 sides
4 angles

Square
4 right angles
4 equal sides

Rectangle
4 right angles
opposite sides equal

Parallelogram
opposite sides equal and parallel

Rhombus
4 equal sides
opposite sides are parallel

Kite
2 pairs of equal sides

Trapezium
one pair of parallel sides

Pentagon	Hexagon	Heptagon
5 sides 5 angles	6 sides 6 angles	7 sides 7 angles
Octagon	**Nonagon**	**Decagon**
8 sides 8 angles	9 sides 9 angles	10 sides 10 angles

Maths ideas

In this unit you will:
* identify and describe two-dimensional shapes
* classify shapes using their properties
* revise the names of circle parts.

Key words

polygon	kite
triangle	trapezium
quadrilateral	circle
square	diameter
rectangle	centre
parallelogram	radius
rhombus	circumference

Circle

Not a polygon

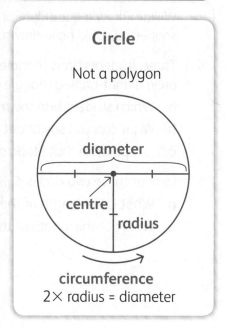

diameter

centre

radius

circumference
2× radius = diameter

1   Explain why each shape is not a polygon.

a   b   c   d

2   Name each polygon as accurately as you can.

a   b   c   d   e

f   g   h   i   j

3   Study the circles.

A   B   C   D

   a   Which of the blue lines show a diameter?
   b   Which of the red lines show a radius?
   c   Which of the green dots are centres of a circle?

Problem-solving

4   William drew a quadrilateral with equal sides. List all the possible shapes he could have drawn.

5   Three students drew triangles. Maria drew a triangle with three angles the same size. Mike drew a right-angled triangle and Jonella drew a triangle with an obtuse angle.
   a   Which student had the triangle with the greatest angle?
   b   What can you say about the other two angles in Mike's triangle?
   c   Is it possible that Maria and Jonella's triangles also had a right angle? Explain your answer.

6   Look at these two circles. O is the centre of both.
   a   What is the length of the radius of the blue circle?
   b   Work out the length of the diameter of each circle.

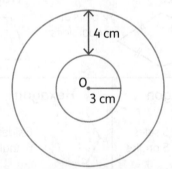

What did you learn?

Draw and label these shapes.

1   A flat shape that is not a polygon

2   A trapezium

3   An obtuse-angled triangle

4   A polygon with four equal sides, but no right angles

C Congruent shapes

Explain

Congruent shapes are exactly the same shape and size.

If you cut out congruent shapes, they will fit exactly on top of each other.

The two shapes in each of these pairs are congruent.

  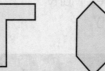 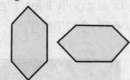

These shapes don't look the same because they aren't all facing the same way, but they are congruent. You can trace them and cut them out to check.

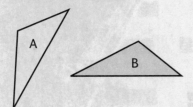 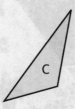 

Maths ideas

In this unit you will:
* learn about congruent shapes
* decide whether shapes are congruent or not.

Key word

congruent

1 In each set of shapes, write the letters of those that are congruent.

a
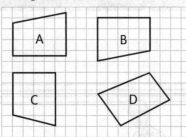

b
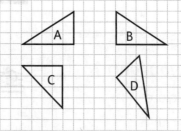

c
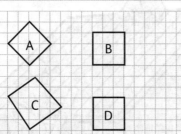

d
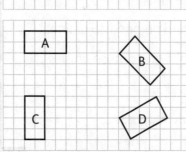

What did you learn?

Are the shapes in each box congruent or not? Give reasons for your answers.

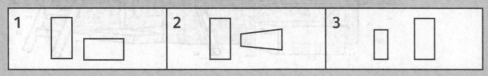

D Shapes around us

Explain

Maths ideas

Geometry is a very old branch of mathematics. 'Geo' means 'earth' and 'metry' means 'measuring'. The word comes from the ancient Egyptians, who had to find ways to measure and mark their fields each year after they were flooded by the Nile river.

Today we use geometry all the time in our daily lives. Many professions also rely on, and make use of, geometry.

In this unit you will:
* explain how people use shapes and geometry in their work and daily lives.

1   Look at this building at Pointe Seraphine in St Lucia. Work in groups and discuss how the designers and builders made use of angles, lines, shapes and congruency in their work.

2   Choose a group of people, for example, artists, craftspeople, engineers, builders, farmers or computer game designers. Prepare a short talk in which you explain why a good understanding of geometry is useful for their work.

What did you learn?

Look at this picture.

Find examples of:

1   parallel and perpendicular lines

2   acute, right and obtuse angles

3   polygons

4   congruent shapes.

Topic 4 review

Key ideas and concepts

Copy the mind map. Draw labelled diagrams to illustrate each concept and summarise what you've learnt in this topic.

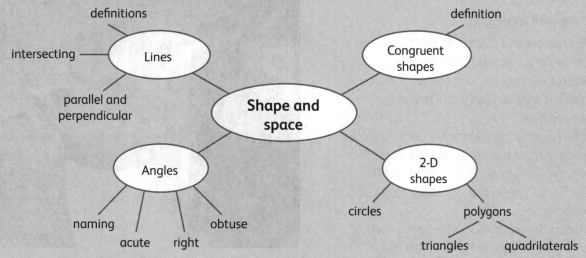

Think, talk, write ...

Everyone uses geometry in some way in their daily lives. Write a short diary entry in your maths journal to explain how you use geometry in the course of a week.

Quick check

1   Study these shapes.

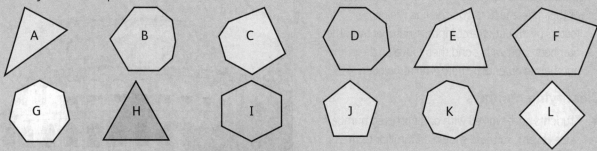

   a   Use the number of sides to name each shape.

   b   Which shape contains only acute angles?

   c   List three shapes that contain at least one right angle.

   d   List three shapes that contain only obtuse angles.

   e   Which shapes have at least two sides that are perpendicular?

   f   Which shapes have at least one pair of parallel sides?

2   Look at this tile pattern. How has the artist used congruency in the design?

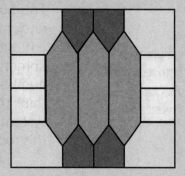

Topic 5 Number sense (2)

Teaching notes

Factors and multiples

* Any number that divides into another without a remainder is a factor of that number.
* The highest common factor of two or more numbers is the greatest factor shared by the numbers.
* When you multiply a whole number by any other whole number, the product is a multiple of that number, for example, $5 \times 1 = 5$, $5 \times 2 = 10$, $5 \times 3 = 15$. The products 5, 10 and 15 are all multiples of 5.
* 10 is the lowest number that is both a multiple of 5 and a multiple of 10, so it is the lowest common multiple of the two sets.

Prime factorisation

* A prime number has only two factors, 1 and the number itself.
* You can write all composite numbers (in other words, numbers that are not prime) as a product of their prime factors. You can find the prime factors by dividing the composite number by prime numbers. Start with 2 and then move up the prime numbers in order until there is no remainder.

Classifying numbers

* Students have worked with odd and even numbers since Level 1, so these should be familiar to them. They also need to recognise square numbers (a number multiplied by itself). It is helpful to memorise the first twelve square numbers.
* Students should recognise the first few prime numbers and be able to work out whether a number (up to 100 at this stage) is a prime number or not.

Roman numerals

* The Roman number system used letters to represent numbers. It did not use place value. Students need to recognise how to read and write low-value Roman numerals. Clock faces with Roman numerals are good for investigating and teaching this.

To park in this lot, you need to pay $3 per hour. What would it cost if you parked for 4 hours? If you have to pay $21 for parking, how many hours was your car parked in the lot?

This building in Rome is what remains of an ancient sports arena called the Colosseum. The entrances are all numbered using the ancient Roman number system. Two gates have the numbers IV and VI on them. What do you think these numbers are in our modern number system? Where do you see numbers written like this today?

Think, talk and write

A Factors and multiples (pages 38–40)

1 What is the product of each of these factor pairs?
a 4 and 9
b 2 and 8
c 4 and 11

2 Read the information and then write your own definition of a factor.

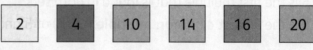
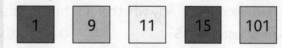

These are all factors of 100: 1, 25, 10, 20
These are not factors of 100: 3, 60, 18, 29

3 Write the next three multiples in each of these sets.
a 3, 6, 9, 12, …
b 25, 50, 75, …
c 10, 20, 30, 40, …
d 11, 22, 33, 44, …

B Classifying numbers (page 41)

Look at these groups of numbers. What can you say about each group?

Group A

| 2 | 4 | 10 | 14 | 16 | 20 |

Group B

| 1 | 9 | 11 | 15 | 101 |

Group C

| 2 | 3 | 5 | 11 | 19 |

Group D

| 15 | 21 | 25 | 50 | 81 |

C Roman numerals (page 42)

Sherie is IX years old and Mark is XI years old.
a How do you know they are not the same age?
b Who is older?
c What is the difference between Sherie and Mark's ages?

Jonella is playing a computer game. She has to drag the numbers on the fish into the correct place in the purple box. The numbers in the box are all in the correct place. Work out how the numbers are grouped. Where will the next two numbers go? Why?

A Factors and multiples

Explain

A **factor** of a number is any whole number that divides into it without a remainder.

7 is a factor of 14 because it divides into 14 twice with no remainder.

7 is also a factor of 28. It divides into 28 four times with no remainder.

All numbers can be divided by 1, so 1 is a factor of every number.

All numbers can also be divided by themselves (to get 1), so every number is a factor of itself.

The factors of 14 are: 1, 2, 7, 14

The factors of 28 are: 1, 2, 4, 7, 14, 28

These two numbers share some of their factors. The highest factor shared by both numbers is 14. 14 is the **highest common factor (HCF)** of 14 and 28.

Multiples of a number are found when you multiply that number by any other whole number.

The first five multiples of 5 are: 5, 10, 15, 20, 25

The first five multiples of 3 are: 3, 6, 9, 12, 15

15 is the first multiple that is found in both sets.

15 is the **lowest common multiple (LCM)** of 5 and 3.

Maths ideas

In this unit you will:
* revise what you learnt last year about factors and multiples
* find the lowest common multiple and highest common factor of sets of numbers
* write numbers as a product of their prime factors.

Key words

factor

highest common factor (HCF)

multiple

lowest common multiple (LCM)

composite numbers

prime numbers

prime factor

product

factor tree

1   Read each statement. Say whether it is true or false.
   a   10 is a factor of 15   b   10 is a factor of 10
   c   12 is a multiple of 6   d   6 is a multiple of 12
   e   1 is a factor of all numbers   f   8 is a factor of 8
   g   1 is a multiple of all numbers   h   8 is a multiple of 8

2   List all the factors of each number in the given set and find the highest common factor.
   a   4 and 6   b   12 and 18   c   10 and 25
   d   3 and 8   e   21 and 49   f   12, 24 and 30
   g   13, 15 and 17   h   6, 10 and 12   i   25, 30 and 40

3   List as many multiples of each number as you need to find the lowest common multiple (LCM) of each set.
   a   4 and 10   b   5 and 6   c   4 and 8
   d   6 and 10   e   9 and 12   f   8 and 20
   g   2, 4 and 5   h   2, 6 and 10   i   8, 9 and 12

Investigate

4   Work in pairs to investigate the numbers from 1 to 100. Use a calculator if you need to. Find out and list the numbers which have:

   a   only one factor
   b   exactly two factors
   c   an even number of factors
   d   an odd number of factors
   e   the highest number of factors.

Challenge

5   Four children all play a computer game on the first day of the year.

   Then Anne plays every second day, Bernard plays every third day, Charles plays every fourth day and Danielle only plays every fifth day.

   a   What is the date when they next all play on the same day?
   b   On how many days of the year do they all play on the same day?

Explain

Numbers that have more than two factors are called **composite numbers**. Composite numbers can be odd or even.
*   16 is a composite number. Its factors are 1, 2, 4, 8 and 16.
*   15 is a composite number. Its factors are 1, 3, 5 and 15.

Numbers that have only two factors are called **prime numbers**.
*   A prime number can only be divided by 1 and itself.
*   5 is a prime number. Its factors are 1 and 5.
*   11 is a prime number. Its factors are 1 and 11.

1 is neither prime nor composite. It is an odd number that has only one factor.
2 is the only even prime number. It has two factors, 1 and 2.
When a factor of any number is also a prime number, it is called a **prime factor**.

Look at the factors of 12: 1, 2, 3, 4, 6, 12.
2 and 3 are factors of 12. They are also prime numbers, so they are prime factors.
Every composite number can be written as a **product** of its prime factors.
You can use a **factor tree** to find the product of prime factors.

Example 1

Write 12 as a product of its prime factors.

Start with any factor pair.
3 is prime. Circle it.
All the circled numbers are prime factors.
Write them as a multiplication.

12 = 2 × 2 × 3

You write the prime factors in ascending order.

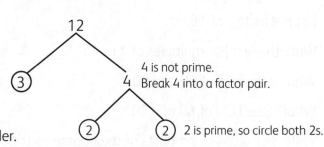

4 is not prime.
Break 4 into a factor pair.

2 is prime, so circle both 2s.

Stop when you cannot break the numbers into factors without using 1.
When you use a factor tree, you can start with any factor pair. You will still end up with the same prime factors.

Example 2

Write 48 as a product of its prime factors.

Method A

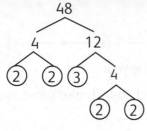

$$48 = 2 \times 2 \times 2 \times 2 \times 3$$

Method B

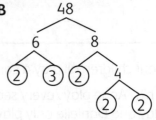

$$48 = 2 \times 2 \times 2 \times 2 \times 3$$

---

6   Use these factor trees to write 50 and 96 as products of their prime factors.

a

b

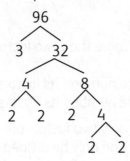

7   Draw your own factor trees to factorise each of these numbers and then write each number as a product of its prime factors.

a   25

b   30

c   18

d   44

e   84

f   64

g   130

h   200

What did you learn?

1   List the factors of 16.

2   Write the first five multiples of 11.

3   What is the HCF of 60 and 80?

4   What is the LCM of 60 and 80?

5   Write 36 and 54 as products of their prime factors.

B Classifying numbers

Explain

Numbers can be grouped, or classified, based on their properties. For example:

* 2 is an **even number** which is also a **prime number**
* 11 is an **odd number** which is also a prime number
* 25 is an odd number which is also **composite** and square
* 32 is an even number which is also composite.

A number multiplied by itself produces a **square number**.

$2 \times 2 = 4$ $3 \times 3 = 9$ $4 \times 4 = 16$

Square numbers have an odd number of factors:

* 25 is a square number. Its factors are 1, 5, 25.
* 16 is a square number. Its factors are 1, 2, 4, 8, 16.

Maths ideas

In this unit you will:
* classify numbers using different properties

Key words

even number

prime number

odd number

composite

square number

1 List:

  a odd numbers between 190 and 220

  b even numbers less than 33

  c odd numbers greater than 60 but less than 83

  d the first five prime numbers

  e composite numbers between 20 and 40.

2 Say whether each statement is true or false.

  a 1 is an odd prime number.

  b All odd numbers are composite.

  c All even numbers except 2 are composite.

  d 2 is the only even prime number.

Problem-solving

3 Work with a partner to solve these number riddles.

I am between 50 and 90. I am an even multiple of 8. 24 is one of my factors.

I am an even number below 79 with the numbers 3, 4 and 5 as some of my factors.

I am even and less than 100. I have an odd number of factors. The sum of my digits is 10.

I am a two-digit prime number less than 20. If you double me and subtract 9, you will get a square number.

I am an odd square number. I am between 20 and 50 and 7 is one of my factors.

What did you learn?

1 How can you tell by looking at a number whether it is odd or even?

2 What is special about prime numbers?

3 How can you tell that the number 1 486 is not prime?

C Roman numerals

Explain

Roman numerals are written using letters to represent numbers.

I = 1   V = 5   X = 10

The Roman number system does not use **place value**.

The letters are combined in different ways to make numbers.

Add the values when the letters are the same.

III = 1 + 1 + 1 = 3   XX = 10 + 10 = 20

Add the values when letters of smaller value are to the right of a letter of greater value.

VII = 5 + 1 + 1 = 7   XII = 10 + 1 + 1 = 12

Subtract the values when letters of smaller value are to the left of a letter of greater value.

IV = 5 − 1 = 4   IX = 10 − 1 = 9

Key words

Roman numeral

place value

1   Look at the clock face with Roman numerals.
    a   What letters are used to make the numbers from 1 to 12?
    b   How are the letters combined to make the numbers?

2   Write these numbers as they would appear in Roman numerals.
    a   5   b   3   c   6   d   7   e   12

3   Write these Roman numerals using ordinary numerals.
    a   XI   b   IX   c   II   d   V   e   VII

Challenge

4   The letters I, V and X are used to write all the Roman numerals up to 49.
    There is a new letter L for 50. How would you write the numbers from 13 to 20
    using the Roman system?

What did you learn?

What is the time on each clock? Write it in numbers.

1
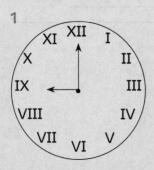

2

3
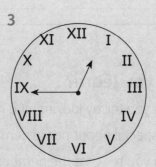

Topic 5 Review

Key ideas and concepts

Write down the correct mathematical term for each statement and give an example to show what each one means.

1   Numbers that have more than two factors

2   Numbers that can be divided by 2 with no remainder

3   A number that will divide into another with no remainder

4   The highest number common to sets of factors

5   Numbers with 1, 2, 3, 5, 7 or 9 in the units position

6   The lowest number in two or more sets of multiples

7   A number that can only be divided equally by itself and 1

8   Products of a number and other numbers

9   Writing a number as a multiplication of factors that are prime numbers

Think, talk, write …

1   Where can you see Roman numerals still being used today?

2   A film made in 2017 has the number MMXVII at the end of it. What does this mean? What can you work out about the letter M? How would you write the current year in Roman numerals?

Quick check

1   List the factors of:

   a   24   b   21   c   13   d   36

2   How do you know from your results in Question 1 that 13 is a prime number?

3   What is the highest common factor of 21, 24 and 36?

4   a   List the first ten multiples of 8.   b   List the first ten multiples of 12.
    c   What is the lowest common multiple of 8 and 12?

5   Here is a set of numbers:

2	8	11	23	25	36	40	49	80	100

   a   List the prime numbers.
   b   List the even composite numbers.
   c   List the square numbers.
   d   Write all the numbers less than 12 in Roman numerals.
   e   Express each composite number as a product of its prime factors.

Problem-solving

6   Micah visits Granny Mavis every fourth Saturday and Granny Celine every third Sunday. He visits them both on the weekend of the 1st and 2nd of March.

   How many weeks will pass until he visits them both on the same weekend again?

Teaching notes

Multiplication and division facts

* Students should know their times tables very well. Continue to skip count in multiples and to drill and practice these regularly. They will use these facts over and over when they multiply and divide in a higher number range.

* The inverse relationship between multiplication and division allows students to use multiplication facts to find related division facts. Continue to generate and use fact families to reinforce this.

Pen-and-paper methods

* Students already know several pen-and-paper methods for multiplying higher numbers and dividing by one-digit numbers. It is important to continue to model multiple calculation strategies. Students should move towards a more formal algorithm only when they are ready to do so.

Long division

* Short division is an important step in developing a good understanding of how division works on paper. Check that students are able to divide using this method, as it is the foundation for the long division algorithm.

* This year, division by two-digit number is introduced as a step-by-step process that relies on place value. It is very important that students line up the numbers as they work down. This way you can reinforce the concept of subtracting tens from tens, hundreds from hundreds, and so on.

* Provide as much support and practice as students need.

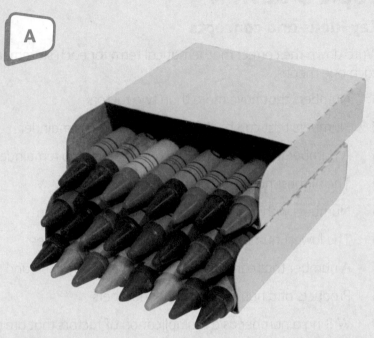

A

Here are 24 crayons. They are arranged in three rows of eight crayons each. Write a multiplication and division fact family using the numbers 3, 8 and 24. If you shared the crayons among 8 children, how many would each child get? How many multiplication facts can you write with a product of 24?

B

We often have to multiply in daily life. The round bread rolls cost 75¢ each and the long ones cost 90¢ each. How much do 4 round rolls cost? What is the cost of 6 long rolls?

1234

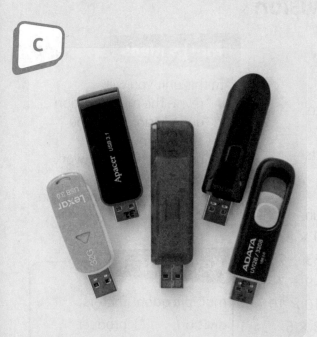

C

Troy bought five thumb drives online for $240. How much did each thumb drive cost? How did you work out the answer?

D

Mrs Carlson hand weaves these patterned strips to make baskets. She uses 7 metres of weaving material to make a large basket. How many metres will she need if she has an order for 25 baskets? If she weaves 135 metres of patterned strips, how many baskets can she make?

Think, talk and write

A **Revisit multiplication and division**
(pages 46–47)

1 Explain how knowing that 6 × 5 = 30 can help you work out that 300 ÷ 6 = 50?

2 Given that 228 ÷ 12 = 19, what is 12 × 19? How do you know that without doing any calculation?

B **Multiplication** (pages 48–49)

1 Look at this number sentence: 32 × 3 = 96. Which one of these statements is correct?
   a 32 is 3 more than 96
   b 32 is 3 times as many as 96
   c 96 is 3 times as many as 32
   d 96 is 32 more than 3

2 How can you double 763 without adding?

C **Division** (pages 50–51)

1 Look at this example.

$$\begin{array}{r} 18\ r\ 3 \\ 4\overline{)7^35} \end{array}$$

2 Which number is:
   a the remainder?
   b the divisor?
   c the quotient?
   d the dividend?

D **Mixed problems** (page 52)

1 How do you know when a problem involves multiplication?

2 How do you know when to divide to solve a problem?

3 What number sentences could you write to solve each of these problems?

> **A** A car uses 8 litres of gas for every 115 km it travels. How many litres of gas would it use to travel 725 km?

> **B** Johnny loves computers and he can type very fast. He estimates that he can type 50 words per minute. How many words is this per half hour?

A Revisit multiplication and division

Multiplication and **division** are **inverse** operations.

You can use multiplication facts to work out division facts.

$12 \times 5 = 60$ So, $60 \div 5 = 12$ and $60 \div 12 = 5$

You can use division facts to work out multiplication facts.

$138 \div 3 = 46$ So, $3 \times 46 = 138$

Maths ideas

In this unit you will:
* revise the multiplication and division facts you already know
* use known facts to work out other facts
* improve your memorisation of times tables.

Key words

multiplication	factors
division	product
inverse	fact family
remainder	

1   Write the answers to these facts as quickly as you can.

a	7×4	b	7×6	c	9×8
d	2×4	e	5×6	f	$63 \div 7$
g	$40 \div 5$	h	$18 \div 3$	i	$49 \div 7$
j	$63 \div 9$	k	5×9	l	10×10
m	7×9	n	4×4	o	3×6
p	$48 \div 4$	q	$12 \div 6$	r	$20 \div 10$
s	$32 \div 8$	t	$15 \div 3$	u	9×9
v	$36 \div 6$	w	$81 \div 9$	x	$56 \div 8$

2   These divisions all leave a **remainder**. How quickly can you write the answers?

a	$22 \div 9$	b	$34 \div 7$	c	$46 \div 6$	d	$58 \div 8$
e	$79 \div 6$	f	$68 \div 9$	g	$81 \div 7$	h	$67 \div 9$
i	$60 \div 7$	j	$65 \div 8$	k	$47 \div 7$	l	$44 \div 6$

3   Choose three **factors** from the box and find their **product**. Can you make 9 different products?

2	3	7	8	10

4   Answer these questions.

   a   How many sixes are there in 63?   b   How can you share 56 evenly among 7 people?

   c   What is $\frac{1}{3}$ of 27?   d   What is 120 divided by 10?

5   For each fact that is given below, write a **fact family** with four related facts.

   a $7 \times 26 = 182$ b $5 \times 39 = 195$ c $234 \div 9 = 26$ d $950 \div 19 = 50$

6   Malia has made some fact family cards. The cards are mixed up and one fact is missing from each family. Find the families and write the missing facts.

$120 \div 4 = 30$	$41 \times 7 = 287$	$588 \div 6 = 98$	$4 \times 147 = 588$
$147 \times 4 = 588$	$6 \times 98 = 588$	$98 \times 6 = 588$	$30 \times 4 = 120$
$7 \times 41 = 287$	$287 \div 7 = 41$	$588 \div 4 = 147$	$120 \div 30 = 4$

7   Find a fact on page 46 to solve each of these problems. Write the answers only.
    a   There are 41 rows of 7 seats. How many seats is this in total?
    b   How many groups of 4 can you make from 120?
    c   An air ticket costs $98.00. If the total cost of tickets is $588.00, how many tickets were purchased?
    d   How many air tickets costing $147.00 each can you buy with $588.00?

8   The area of a rectangle is its length multiplied by its width. What is the area of each of these rectangles?

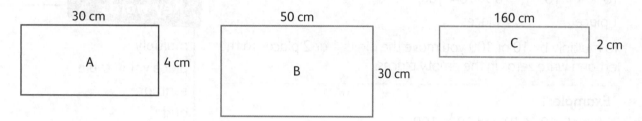

9   The area of these rectangles is given. Work out the missing side length.

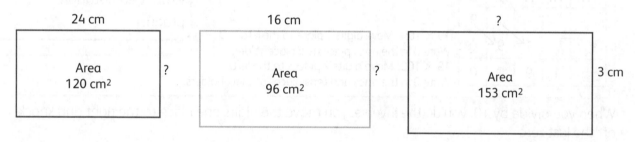

Problem-solving

10 Mrs Smith does these exercises every morning before work:
    ✳   10 press ups
    ✳   9 sit ups
    ✳   8 step ups
    ✳   7 star jumps
    ✳   6 stretches.

    How many of each exercise does Mrs Smith do in one week?

What did you learn?

$6 \times 8 = a$ $6 \times b = 48$ $c \times 8 = 48$

1   What are the values of a, b and c?

2   Which operation did you use to find b and c? Why?

3   If $x \div 6 = 9$, what would you do to find the value of x? Why?

B Multiplication

Explain

Do you remember how to **multiply** by 10 and 100?

You know that each place on the **place value table** is 10 times greater than the value to its right. You can use this fact to find quick methods of multiplying by 10 and 100.

$10 \times 1 = 10$ $10 \times 10 = 100$

1 place   2 places

To multiply by 10 or 100 you move the digits 1 or 2 places to the left and write zeros in the empty places.

Example 1

Multiply 19×10 and 19×100.

TTh	Th	H	T	O
			1	9
		1	9	0
	1	9	0	0

19×10:   Move digits 1 place to the left.
Write 0 in the ones place as a placeholder.
19×100: Move digits 2 places to the left.
Write 0 in the ones and tens places as placeholders.

When you divide by 10, you do the inverse: you move the digits one place to the right and knock off the last zero.

$190 \div 10 = 19$.

This can help you **estimate** when you use numbers rounded to the nearest 10 or 100.

Example 2

300×6 Think of this as $3 \times 100 \times 6$

$3 \times 6 = 18$

$18 \times 100 = 1\,800$

You also learnt how to multiply larger numbers last year using the **grid** method and the **long multiplication** method. Read through these examples to revise these two methods of working.

Example 3

Grid method   Calculate 148×23.

Estimate: $150 \times 20 = 150 \times 10 \times 2 = 1\,500 \times 2 = 3\,000$

×	20	3	
100	2 000	300	→ 2 300
40	800	120	→ 920
8	160	24	→ 184
			3 404

Write the number in **expanded notation** on the grid.

Multiply to fill each cell.

Add the totals in each row to get the product.

Long multiplication method   Calculate 148 × 23.
Estimate: 150 × 20 = 150 × 10 × 2 = 1 500 × 2 = 3 000

```
      148
    × 23
 ────────
      24      (3 × 8)      Multiply each digit in the top number by 3. Remember the place values.
    1
     120      (3 × 40)
     300      (3 × 100)
     160      (20× 8)      Then multiply each digit in the top number by 20.
     800      (20 × 40)
   1
   2 000    (20 × 100)
 ────────
   3 404                   Add to find the product.
 ────────
```

1   Multiply.
    a   25 × 20   b   68 × 40   c   80 × 30   d   124 × 30
    e   112 × 40   f   47 × 20   g   64 × 10   h   700 × 30

2   Estimate and then calculate the products. Use the method that you find most efficient.
    a   234 × 65   b   220 × 48   c   378 × 14   d   297 × 70
    e   534 × 75   f   98 × 322   g   903 × 66   h   12 × 350

Problem-solving

3   There are 24 bottles in a crate. How many bottles will there be in 368 crates?

4   A family saves $245.00 per month. How much will they save in a year?

5   Bananas are transported from the farm to the packing plant by truck. Each truck carries 576 hands of bananas.
    a   The mean mass of a hand of bananas is 480 grams. What is the mean mass carried by each truck?
    b   How many bananas are carried by 14 trucks if they each make two trips?

6   A factory makes 321 T-shirts per week. How many will they make in a year if they close down for 3 weeks each summer?

7   Kayla calculates that she takes 960 steps to get to school and back each day. How many steps will she take to school and back in four weeks?

8   A school principal lives 11 km from school. During a year, she travels to school and back about 275 times. Work out how many kilometres this is in total.

What did you learn?

Find the product.

1   41 and 24   2   65 and 14   3   158 and 18   4   124 and 34

C Division

Explain

Last year, you learnt how to **divide** by a 1-digit **divisor** using a division house symbol and carrying numbers. Remember that if the **dividend** (the number you divide into) is not in the times table, you can still find the **quotient** using a written method called short **division**. Here are two examples to remind you how to do this.

$$
\begin{array}{r} 14 \\ 9\overline{)12^36} \end{array}
\qquad
\begin{array}{r} 17\,r\,3 \\ 7\overline{)12^59} \end{array}
\qquad 7 \times 8 = 56
$$

When you divide by a two-digit number, it is easier to keep track of your working if you use a longer method of writing out your calculations. Look at these two examples to see how to do this.

Maths ideas

In this unit you will:
* use pen-and-paper methods to perform short and long division
* solve problems that involve division.

Key words

divide	quotient
divisor	division
dividend	remainder

Example 1

$249 \div 21$ Estimate: $200 \div 20 = 10$

Step 1:

$$
\begin{array}{r} 1 \\ 21\overline{)249} \\ -21 \\ \hline 3 \end{array}
$$

Divide the tens
$21 \times 1 = 21$
Subtract $24 - 21 = 3$
21 cannot go into 3

Step 2:

$$
\begin{array}{r} 11\,r\,18 \\ 21\overline{)249} \\ -21\downarrow \\ \hline 39 \\ 21 \\ \hline 18 \end{array}
$$

Bring down the ones
Divide
$21 \times 2 = 42$ ✗ too high
$21 \times 1 = 21$
Subtract $39 - 21 = 18$
$18 < 21$, so it is the **remainder**

Example 2

$1\,376 \div 12$ Estimate: $1\,000 \div 10 = 100$

$$
\begin{array}{r} 114\,r\,8 \\ 12\overline{)1\,376} \\ -12\downarrow \\ \hline 17 \\ -12 \\ \hline 56 \\ -48 \\ \hline 8 \end{array}
$$

Bring down the tens
Bring down the ones
$12 \times 4 = 48$
Subtract $56 - 48 = 8$
$8 < 12$, so it is the remainder

This method is called long division.

1 Divide.

　a 369 ÷ 3　　　b 484 ÷ 4　　　c 204 ÷ 4　　　d 690 ÷ 6

　e 324 ÷ 6　　　f 808 ÷ 8　　　g 516 ÷ 6　　　h 432 ÷ 8

　i 261 ÷ 2　　　j 362 ÷ 3　　　k 481 ÷ 8　　　l 8 435 ÷ 7

2 Estimate and then calculate. Show your working.

　a 868 ÷ 15　　b 636 ÷ 21　　c 906 ÷ 52　　d 456 ÷ 16

　e 987 ÷ 41　　f 843 ÷ 27　　g 1 152 ÷ 12　　h 6 578 ÷ 11

3 Use long division to find the quotients.

　a 3 412 ÷ 15　　b 6 712 ÷ 31　　c 9 873 ÷ 18　　d 1 235 ÷ 24

　e 2 346 ÷ 21　　f 1 987 ÷ 23　　g 96 713 ÷ 17　　h 28 856 ÷ 12

　i 10 821 ÷ 19　　j 79 778 ÷ 14　　k 20 095 ÷ 36　　l 79 073 ÷ 12

Problem-solving

4 For a concert, chairs were arranged in rows of 15. If there were 360 chairs, how many rows were there?

5 The mass of 37 sacks of cement is 3 885 kg. What is the mass of one bag?

6 Ms Dorleon is running a virus check on her computer. The display shows this information:

Progress
Status: Scan progressing …
Product: Fraud.Sysguard
Estimated time left: 14365 minutes

　a How many hours will the virus check take?

　　She looks again later and the display shows this information:

Progress
Status: Scan progressing…
Product: Fraud.Sysguard
Estimated time left: 5414 minutes

　b How much time has passed (in hours) from the first display to the second?

What did you learn?

Divide.

1 1 520 ÷ 10

2 495 ÷ 5

3 336 ÷ 16

4 7 750 ÷ 25

D Mixed problems

Work with a partner. Read through the problems and talk about what you will need to do to solve each one. Then work on your own to find the answer using **multiplication**, **division** or both. Show your workings.

Maths ideas

In this unit you will:
* apply what you know to solve problems involving multiplication and division.

1   What is the **quotient** and **remainder** if the **product** of 168 and 46 is divided by 29?

2   Work out the missing digits in this calculation.

    263 × 4__ = 11 8__5

3   Tony has 2 462 elastic bands. He packs these into boxes each containing 80 elastic bands. How many boxes can he fill? How many elastic bands will be left over?

Key words

multiplication   remainder
division   product
quotient

4   Sharyn has 320 points. Andy has 100 times as many. How many does Andy have?

5   A rectangle is ten times as long as it is wide. If it is 23 cm wide, calculate its area.

6   A ferry across Pirate Bay costs $2.00. If there are 35 passengers per trip and the ferry crosses 9 times, how much money will they have collected in ticket fees?

7   Mrs Norris can pack mangoes into bags containing 12, 14, 15, 16, 18 or 20 mangoes. Which size bag is best for 1 265 mangoes so that the fewest possible mangoes will be left over?

8   A pilot flies 856 km a week. If she works 48 weeks of the year, what distance does she fly in all?

9   5 256 tickets costing $23.00 each are sold for a cricket final. What is the total cost?

10 768 students and 25 teachers are to be transported to an event by bus. Each bus can safely carry 32 passengers. How many buses will be needed to transport everyone?

What did you learn?

1   It costs a fisherman $165 per week to moor his boat in the harbour. What is the cost per year?

2   The fisherman caught 358 fish over a certain period. He sold the fish for an average price of $24.00 each. How much money did he receive from the sale of the fish?

Weekly mooring fee: $165

Topic 6 Review

Key ideas and concepts

To complete this diagram, go back through the units in this topic. For each one, write down the main things you learnt.

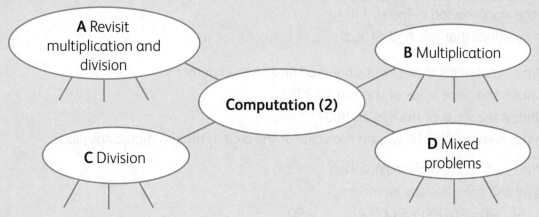

Think, talk, write

1   Think about the fact family for 132, 12 and 1 584.
   a   Which numbers are factors?   b   What number is a product?
   c   Which numbers can be used as divisors?   d   Which numbers are quotients?

2   Make up three multiplication and three division story problems. Exchange your story problems with another student and solve each other's problems.

Quick check

1   Which student's answer is correct for each multiplication?

Calculation	Fabian	Lucien	Veronique
27 × 332	12 284	8 964	9 000
495 × 18	8 910	10 710	89 100
722 × 12	8 466	0 664	8 664
119 × 21	2 550	2 450	2 499
495 × 68	33 606	31 212	333 660

2   Divide. Show your workings.
   a   235 ÷ 12   b   423 ÷ 18   c   12 456 ÷ 23

Problem-solving

3   5 326 people are invited to a function. There are 18 seats at each table. How many tables will be needed?

4   How many lengths of 19 m can you cut from a piece of rope that is 2 000 m long?

Test yourself (1)

Explain

Complete this test to check that you have understood and can manage the work covered in Topics 1 to 6.
Revise any sections that you find difficult.

1   a   Write twenty-nine thousand six hundred and three in numerals.
    b   What is the place value of the 9 in 49 328?
    c   What is the value of the 8 in 74 860?
    d   In the numeral 65 318, what is the value of the digit in the ten thousands place?

2   a   Write 72 518 in expanded notation.
    b   Copy and complete the equations.
        i   56 390 = 50 000 + 6 000 + _____ + 90
        ii 36 419 = 3 × 10 000 + 6 × 1 000 + _____ × 100 + 1 × _____ + 9 × 1

3   Round 10 649 to the nearest thousand.

4   Arrange these numbers in order from least to greatest.

    8 013, 8 113, 801, 80 999, 81 000

5   The difference between two numbers is 57. If one of the numbers is 38, what is the other number?

6   There are 65 fewer plums than cherries in a box. There are 216 cherries in the box. How many plums are there?

7   James has 47 crayons. Jim has twice as many as James. David has 13 crayons more than James. How many crayons do the three boys have altogether?

8   James can wash 6 cars per hour. He is paid $20 for washing each car. How many hours will he take to earn $480?

9   The sum of two numbers is 3 458. If the smaller number is 1 567, what is the larger number?

10 You are given the numbers 1 937 and 573. Estimate the sum of the two numbers and explain the strategy you used.

11 What is the next time at which the hands on the clock below will make a right angle?

12 What do you call an angle that is smaller than 90°?

13 Draw and label a line segment AB, which is 6 cm long.

14 Which statement below is true about rectangle ABCD?

   a   AB is parallel to BC.

   b   AD is perpendicular is DC.

   c   DC is a vertical line.

15 What is the correct name for a plane shape with opposite and adjacent sides equal in length and four angles, each measuring 90°?

16 Read the description. Then draw and name the shape.

> I have 4 sides. 2 opposite sides are long and 2 opposite sides are short. I am flat with 2 lines of symmetry.

17 Draw a circle. Indicate and label the diameter, radius, circumference and centre.

18 Complete this sentence: These triangles are congruent because …

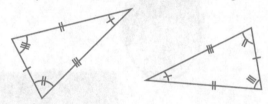

19 Use the numbers in the box to complete each statement that follows. Each number can only be used once.

18	0	12	2	7

   a _____ and _____ are prime numbers.

   b The lowest common multiple of 6 and 9 is _____.

   c _____ is both even and composite.

   d This whole number is not odd nor even nor prime: _____.

20 a Write 36 as a product of its prime factors.

   b Which of these is not a factor of 18?   5   6   9

   c What is the highest common factor (HCF) of 16 and 24?

   d What is the lowest common multiple (LCM) of 4, 6 and 8?

   e A vendor wants to pack marbles into bags containing 3, 4 or 6. What is the fewest number of marbles that would be needed to do this?

21 Find the product of 77 and 40.

22 How many times can 11 be taken from 143?

23 A full bus carries 15 children. A group of 63 children are to be taken on a tour. How many buses are needed to carry ALL the children?

24 Write 11 using Roman numerals.

Topic 7 Measurement (1)

Teaching notes

Metric units

* The units in the metric system work in multiples of 10 and allow you to write measurements in equivalent ways.
* Students need to realise that when they convert to a bigger unit (for example, from grams to kilograms) they will have a smaller number of that unit, and when they convert to a smaller unit they will have a larger number of those units.

Mass

* Explain to students that we often talk about the 'weight' of something when we really mean the 'mass'. While we may say 'I weigh 40 kilograms', mass and weight are technically not the same.
* Grams and milligrams are small units of mass. It is important to give students lots of practical measuring tasks so they can develop a sense of mass and learn to read the scale on various measuring instruments.

Capacity

* Students have already learnt about capacity and have estimated and measured liquids in litres and centilitres. Remind them that the capacity of a container is a measure of how much it can hold in total. When a container is partly filled, we talk about the volume of liquid it contains.
* Continue to work with concrete objects when estimating and measuring capacity.

Length

* Students need ongoing and regular practice to estimate and measure accurately. Help students improve their skills by working with concrete objects and real-life situations. Use measuring instruments marked in different units to encourage converting between these.

Scale drawings

* Scale drawings are representations of the real world in which everything is drawn at the same fraction of its actual size.
* Maps are good examples of scale drawings. The line scales on maps can be used to find real-world distances. Make sure that your students understand that measurements on the line scale show the real-life distances represented that the small divisions represent. So a 1 cm division on a map scale can have a label that states that 1 cm represents 250 metres.

A

We use scales to measure mass. Which of these kinds of scales have you seen or used? What everyday items can you weigh using each kind of scale? Can you explain how each scale works?

B

These bottles all have a capacity of $1\frac{1}{2}$ litres. What does this mean? Which bottle is almost filled to capacity? Estimate how much liquid is in each bottle. Can you give your answers in a different unit?

C

What units of length are shown on the diagram of the ruler? What do the smaller lines between the numbers show? Use the diagram to estimate the width of the pencil point and the crayon point and the diameter of the pencil eraser.

Think, talk and write

A   Mass *(pages 58–59)*

1   Work in groups. Each group will need a crayon and a book.
   a   Find two items that have about the same mass as the crayon.
   b   Find two items that have about the same mass as the book.
   c   Find something that is lighter than the crayon.
   d   Find something that is heavier than the book.

2   Which units would you use to measure the mass of these items?
   a   Light items such as a piece of paper or a pen.
   b   Heavier items such as a table or chair.

B   Capacity *(pages 60–61)*

1   Do tall containers always have a greater capacity than shorter containers? Explain your answer.

2   Think about your own home.
   a   Which container in your home holds the most liquid?
   b   What containers hold more than 2 litres?
   c   What is the smallest container of liquid? What shape is it?

C   Length *(pages 62–64)*

1   Work in groups. Estimate the height of each person in your group. Then use a metre rule or tape measure to measure each person's height. Work out the difference between the estimated and actual heights.

2   What is the most appropriate unit to measure these?
   a   The distance from one end of an island to the other end.
   b   The thickness of a passport.
   c   The length of an airplane.
   d   The distance from the arrivals lounge at the airport to the parking area at the airport.
   e   The height of a stop sign in the airport parking area.

3   What is a scale drawing?

A Mass

Explain

You already know how to measure the **mass** of items using different **units**.

The standard unit of measurement for mass is the **gram** (g). A large paperclip weighs about 1 gram (g). Some things are even lighter than this. We measure them in **milligrams** (mg). We measure heavier things in **kilograms** (kg) and **tonnes** (t).

These units form part of the **metric system** of measurement.

1 g = 1 000 mg   1 kg = 1 000 g   1 t = 1 000 kg

You can **convert** measurements from one unit to another.

* When you convert from a larger unit to a smaller unit, you will get a bigger number of units.
* When you convert from a smaller unit to a larger unit, you will get a smaller number of units.

Example 1

5 kg = _____ g

There are 1 000 g in 1 kg.

5 kg = 5 × 1 000 g

So, 5 kg = 5 000 g

Example 2

2 500 g = _____ kg

There are 1 000 g in 1 kilogram.

2 500 g = 1 000 g + 1 000 g + 500 g

= 1 kg + 1 kg + $\frac{1}{2}$ kg

So, 2 500 g = $2\frac{1}{2}$ kg

Maths ideas

In this unit you will:
* estimate and measure mass in kilograms, grams and milligrams
* compare the mass of different objects using different units of measurements.

Key words

mass	kilogram
units	tonne
gram	metric system
milligram	convert

Think and talk

Do larger objects always have a greater mass than smaller objects? Give reasons for your answer.

---

1   Choose the most reasonable mass for each object.

a   a lettuce leaf

2 g or 2 kg?

b   a pickup truck

100 kg or 1 000 kg?

c   a whole mango

120 g or 120 mg?

d   a schoolbag full of books

30 g or 3 kg?

e   one tablet

500 mg or 500 g?

f   a bag of oranges

500 kg or 5 kg?

g   a block of butter

$\frac{1}{2}$ kg or $\frac{1}{2}$ g?

h   a slice of bread

50 g or 50 mg?

i   a hand of bananas

500 g or 5 kg?

2 Leroy drew this diagram to help him convert between units of mass. How does it work?

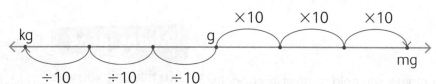

3 Convert these measurements. Use a diagram like Leroy's if you find it helpful.

a 3 g = _____ mg   b 2 kg = _____ g   c 4 000 mg = _____ g

d 2 000 mg = _____ g   e 5 000 g = _____ kg   f 30 g = _____ mg

4 Express the following masses in grams.

a 3 kg   b $2\frac{1}{2}$ kg   c $5\frac{1}{4}$ kg   d 6 kg 100 g

5 Express these masses in kilograms.

a 4 500 g   b 7 750 g   c 19 000 g   d 11 250 g

Problem-solving

6 Solve these word problems. Show your workings.

a James needs to move books from his classroom to the library. The total mass of the books is 45 kg. He has a crate that can take at most 8 kg at a time. How many trips must he make?

b A farm produces 35 000 kg of mangoes. They sell the mangoes in boxes of 5 kg to the supermarkets. How many boxes can they make?

c A packet of flour has a mass of $2\frac{1}{2}$ kg. The baker uses 250 g for each batch of muffins. How many batches can she make from one packet?

Challenge

7 Mr Jones bought $2\frac{1}{2}$ kg of beef, 3 kg 700 g of pork and 4 kg 800 g of lamb. What was the total mass of the meat in kilograms?

8 The average mass of a human brain is 1 kg 350 g, the average mass of an elephant's brain is 5 kg 400 g and the mass of a whale's brain is 9 kg.

a What is the difference in mass between a human brain and a whale's brain?

b How much heavier is a whale's brain than an elephant's brain?

What did you learn?

1 Arrange each set of masses in descending order.

a 5 kg $12\frac{1}{2}$ kg $2\frac{1}{4}$ kg   3 000 g   10 000 mg

b 150 g   1 kg   7 500 mg   2 kg $\frac{1}{2}$ kg

2 Convert these masses to grams.

a 2 kg   b $3\frac{1}{4}$ kg

3 Create two of your own word problems involving g or kg. Work them out and explain how you reached the answer.

B Capacity

The amount of liquid that a container can hold is called its **capacity**. We can use **litres** (ℓ), **centilitres** (cℓ) and smaller units called **millilitres** (mℓ) to measure how much liquid a container holds.

1 litre (1ℓ) = 100 centilitres (cℓ)

1 litre (1ℓ) = 1 000 millilitres (mℓ)

1 centilitre is equivalent to 10 millilitres

When a container is not filled to capacity we talk about the **volume** of liquid it contains.

In everyday life, we often use other more informal units of capacity. When you work with recipes, you will find capacity given in cups and spoons.

Here are the metric equivalents of cups and spoons:

1 teaspoon (tsp) = 5 mℓ

1 tablespoon (tbsp) = 15 mℓ

1 metric cup = 250 mℓ

$\frac{1}{2}$ cup = 125 mℓ

$\frac{1}{4}$ cup = $62\frac{1}{2}$ mℓ (usually rounded to 60 mℓ)

Maths ideas

In this unit you will:
* estimate and measure capacity in litres, centilitres and millilitres
* compare the capacity of different containers using different units of measurement.

Key words

capacity

litre (ℓ)

centilitre (cℓ)

millilitre (mℓ)

volume

1 a Collect a range of bottles, cups and jars.

   b Arrange them in order, from those that seem to hold the least to those that seem to hold the most liquid. Give each container a letter: A, B, C, D, and so on.

   c Write the capacity (in mℓ or ℓ) of each container. Measure it using water and a measuring jug if it does not have a label.

   d Was your order in part **b** correct?

   e Convert the capacities so that you have recorded them in millilitres and litres.

2 Read the recipe for this sauce. Write the measurement for each ingredient in millilitres.

Chocolate sauce

$\frac{3}{4}$ cup sugar

$1\frac{1}{4}$ cup milk

$1\frac{1}{2}$ tbsp flour

2 tbsp butter

$\frac{1}{2}$ cup cocoa powder

$\frac{1}{2}$ tsp vanilla extract

Sift the sugar, flour and cocoa together.

Heat the milk, butter and vanilla in a small pot until the butter melts.

Whisk the cocoa mixture into the pot.

Bring it to the boil and cook for 6 minutes.

Pour the sauce over ice-cream.

---

3 a Mila needs 2 ℓ of milk to make pancakes for a school fair. The store only has milk in containers of 25 cℓ. How many must she buy?

   b Noah buys 8 ℓ of juice for a party. There will be 20 guests, and he wants to make sure there is enough for each guest to have at least two cups of juice. How much more juice must he buy?

   c A chef makes 1.5 ℓ of apple sauce to use in apple pies. Each pie needs $\frac{1}{2}$ cup of apple sauce. How many pies can she make altogether with the apple sauce?

4 Look at this recipe.

Sweet and Sour Sauce (makes $1\frac{1}{2}$ cups)

1 cup pineapple juice $\frac{1}{2}$ cup brown sugar

1 tbsp soya sauce   3 tbsp vinegar

$\frac{1}{3}$ cup water   3 tbsp cornstarch

Mix all the ingredients together and cook over low heat until thickened.

Serve over chicken or vegetables and rice.

---

   a Express all the quantities in millilitres.

   b Calculate how much you would need of each ingredient to make double the quantity.

5 Write three questions of your own about measuring capacity. In groups, put together your questions to make a booklet of problems. Exchange booklets with another group and solve each other's questions.

What did you learn?

1 How many litres are there in:
   a 24 cups?   b 4 cups?   c 4 500 mℓ?   d 400 cℓ?

2 Write these volumes in litres.
   a 5 000 mℓ   b 1 500 cℓ   c 4 500 mℓ   d 13 250 mℓ

3 Which of these three jars would best fit this curry mixture?

5 tbsp ground coriander   1 tsp cinnamon

2 tbsp ground cumin $\frac{1}{2}$ tsp cloves

1 tbsp ground turmeric $\frac{1}{2}$ tsp ground cardamom

2 tsp ground ginger $\frac{1}{2}$ tsp ground chilli peppers

2 tsp dry mustard

$1\frac{1}{2}$ tsp black pepper

  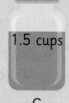

$\frac{1}{2}$ cup   1 cup   1.5 cups

A   B   C

C Length

Length is a measure of how long, wide, tall or far something is.
Length, **width**, **height** and **distance** are all types of length.

You can measure short lengths in **centimetres** (cm),
millimetres (mm) or a combination of both.

Remember: 1 cm = 10 mm and $\frac{1}{2}$ cm = 5 mm.

The length of this royal gramma fish
can be written in different ways.

Look at the ruler.

The fish is $3\frac{1}{2}$ cm long.

This is the same as 35 millimetres.

You can also write this as 3 cm 5 mm.

Longer lengths and distances are usually measured in **metres**
and **kilometres**.

1 metre = 100 centimetres and 1 kilometre = 1 000 metres.

Maths ideas

In this unit you will:
* estimate and measure
  lengths in metres,
  centimetres and millimetres
* compare the length and
  height of different objects
  using different units of
  measurement
* learn about scale
  drawings and how they
  are used in daily life
* use the scale on a diagram
  to work out real-life lengths
* make your own
  scale diagrams.

Key words

length	estimate
width	measure
height	scale diagram
distance	map
centimetre	plan
millimetre	scale
metre	fraction
kilometres	bar scale

1   **Estimate** and then **measure** the length of each of these fish.
    Write each length in three ways: in centimetres, in millimetres
    and in a combination of centimetres and millimetres.

    a   b   c

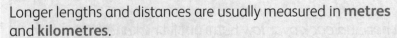

    d   e

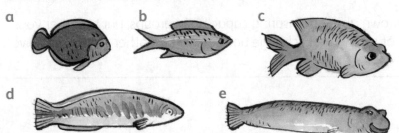

2   Draw these straight-line segments.
    a   AB = 55 mm   b   CD = 8 cm   c   EF = $7\frac{1}{2}$ cm   d   GH = 2 cm 8 mm

3   Work with a partner. Estimate and then measure these objects:
    a   the dimensions (marked A to D) of a chair in centimetres
    b   the length, width and thickness of this maths book in millimetres
    c   the longest distance in your classroom in metres.

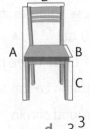

4   Convert each of these measurements to centimetres.
    a $1\frac{1}{2}$ m   b   2 m   c $2\frac{1}{4}$ m   d $3\frac{3}{4}$ m

5   Write each height in metres and centimetres.
    a   430 cm   b   250 cm   c   575 cm   d   609 cm

6   Write each of these measurements in centimetres and then convert each one to millimetres.
    a   2 m 40 cm   b   3 m 10 cm   c   4 m 1 cm   d   1 m 73 cm

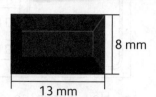

7 A block of chocolate is 8 mm wide and 13 mm long. A slab has 8 rows of blocks.

    a How long is the whole slab?

    b What other information would we need to work out how wide the slab is?

8 A wooden plank is 15 mm thick. I have a stack of 8 planks.

    a How high is the stack?

    b I place the stack on a shelf that is 25 cm below the shelf above it. How many more planks can I fit on the stack before the shelf is full?

Scale diagrams

Explain

A **scale diagram** is an accurate drawing that shows something at a smaller size than it really is. **Maps** and **plans** are scale diagrams of the real world.

The **scale** on a map or plan compares the size of the diagram with the size of the real thing that is shown.

Scale can be given in words. For example: 1 cm = 120 cm. This means one centimetre on the diagram is equivalent to 120 cm in the real world. The diagram is a **fraction** of the size of the real thing, in this case $\frac{1}{120}$th of the real size. Scale can also be given as a bar. **Bar scales** are often found on maps.

Example 1

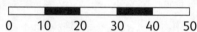

| 0 | 10 | 20 | 30 | 40 | 50 |

1 cm on this map (the length of a section of the bar) is equivalent to 50 km in the real world. We can use the scale to work out real distances.

Example 2

What is the actual length of this phone? And what is its width?

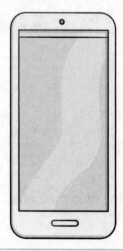

Scale: 1 cm = $2\frac{1}{2}$ cm

Length on diagram = 6 cm

So real length is $6 \times 2\frac{1}{2}$ cm

6×25 mm = 150 mm or 15 cm

Width on diagram = 3 cm

So real length is $3 \times 2\frac{1}{2}$ cm

3×25 mm = 75 mm or $7\frac{1}{2}$ cm

The real phone is 150 mm long and 75 mm wide.

9 This scale drawing of a microwave oven has a scale of 1 cm to 12 cm.

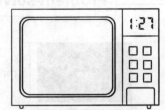

    a How high is the real oven?

    b What is the length and width of the door of the real oven?

10 Use this map of the route of a car journey to answer the questions.

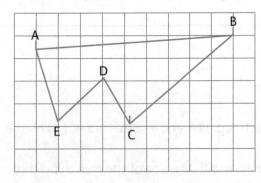

			km
0	12	24

    a What is the real distance from A to B along the straight line?

    b What is the real distance from B to D?

    c How much further do you have to travel to A once you reach point D?

Think and talk

How would you make an accurate scale drawing of your classroom? Write down the steps you would follow.

What did you learn?

1 Copy and complete. Use <, = or >.

    a 18 cm ☐ 180 mm

    b $4\frac{1}{2}$ m ☐ 425 cm

    c 2 m ☐ 300 cm

2 A tree is 850 cm tall. How tall is this in metres?

3 Write the name of an object that has a length of approximately:

    a 2 m

    b 2 cm

    c 2 mm

    d 2 km

4 A distance of 1 cm on a map is equivalent to 25 km in reality. A road on the map measures $2\frac{1}{2}$ cm. How long is this road in the real world?

5 Explain why a car in a photograph appears much smaller than it really is.

Topic 7 Review

Key ideas and concepts

Answer these questions to summarise what you learnt in this topic.

1 What units can you use to measure longer distances? What is the relationship between them?

2 What would you measure in kilograms?

3 How many grams are there in 3 kilograms?

4 What does a capacity of 3 litres mean?

5 What is the difference between a scale on a measuring jug and a scale on a map?

6 Give three real-life examples of scale diagrams and how are they used.

Think, talk, write …

1 Make a list of jobs in which people use measurement regularly. Give one example of how each person might use measurement in each job.

2 Use an atlas and a map of South America to work out:
   a how wide South America is at its widest point.
   b the real distance from Caracas to Georgetown.

Quick check

1 Name three metric units used for measuring mass.

2 Which of the following might have a mass of 72 kg: a baby, a car, or a man?

3 Which of the following might have a mass of 120 g: a textbook, an apple, or a pen?

4 Write these measurements in grams.
   a $\frac{1}{2}$ kg
   b 2 kg
   c $5\frac{1}{4}$ kg

5 Write these measurements in kilograms.
   a 1 000 g
   b 8 500 g
   c 4 250 g

6 How many:
   a millilitres are in half a litre?
   b cups are in 2 litres?

Problem-solving

7 Leroy decides to go on a weight loss plan. His starting mass is 123 kg. He aims to lose 500 g per week. His target mass is 90 kg. How long will it take him to reach his target mass?

8 A frog jumps 23 cm with each jump.
   a How many jumps does it take for the frog to cover more than 2 m?
   b After the last jump, what is the total distance the frog has covered?

9 Draw a scale diagram of a rectangular field that is 40 m long and 25 m wide. Use a scale of 1 cm = 5 m. Draw a bar scale for the diagram.

Topic 8
Data handling (1)

Teaching notes

Methods of collecting data

* Students already know how to collect data by doing observations, drawing up a questionnaire and conducting an interview.
* Observation involves looking and often counting. A questionnaire is a form that is used to collect and record data. An interview involves asking questions to collect data.
* Students need to think carefully about what they are trying to find out to choose the most appropriate method for collecting the data. At this level, data sets are fairly uncomplicated and the samples are small, so students can generally choose the method they think is best quite easily. In the real world, time, budgets and sample sizes make these decisions more complicated.

Organising data

* Sets of numbers are not really useful or easy to interpret. Data is more useful if it is sorted and organised.
* A frequency table is a way of organising data to show how many (the frequency) data items there are in each category or group.
* Some tables combine tally marks and frequencies.

Averages

* Averages give you a general idea of what a data set tells you, for example, the average salary of office workers, or the average time a student spends watching TV each night.
* There are different types of average, but students only need to work with the mean. The mean is an arithmetic average: students first find the sum of the data values and then divide the answer by the number of data items.

A

How would you collect and organise data about which colour car is most common in your community? Would you use the same method to find out which type of car people would like to own? Explain why or why not.

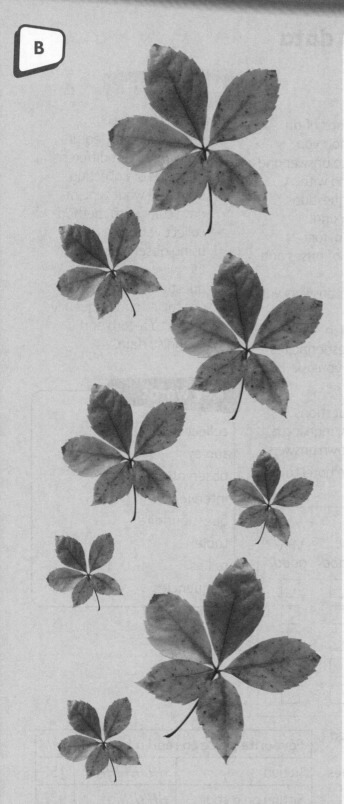

These leaves all come from the same tree. A scientist wants to describe them and she says, 'this tree produced leaves that are 50 mm long on average'. Do you think this means all the leaves are 50 mm long? Why or why not? How do you think she decided on this length?

Think, talk and write

A   Collecting and organising data
(pages 68–70)

1   Read these questions and discuss with your group how you could find the data you need to answer them.

> How many brothers and sisters do students in my level have?

> Should our town's streets be closed to traffic on Saturdays so that market stalls can be set up?

> How many students at my school need glasses or contact lenses?

2   How can a table help you organise the data you collect?

B   Averages – the mean *(pages 71–72)*

1   The average temperature for each month of the year in St Lucia is given in the table.

Average temperature in St Lucia

Jan	Feb	Mar	Apr	May	Jun
24	24	25	26	28	30

Jul	Aug	Sep	Oct	Nov	Dec
31	31	30	29	26	25

a   Are these temperatures in degrees Celsius or Fahrenheit? How do you know?

b   What is the difference in temperature between the hottest and coolest months?

c   How do you think the weather office finds these figures for average temperature?

A Collecting and organising data

Explain

You already know that you can **collect data** by means of an interview, a questionnaire or observation. The method you choose will depend on the question you are trying to answer and the number of pieces of information you are working with. A **survey** is any method of collecting data by asking questions.

* When you find the answers you need by looking and counting, you are doing a survey by **observation**, for example, if you observe and record the number of buses and trucks passing an intersection.

* When you ask people questions and record their answers you are doing an **interview**.

* When you use a form that you give people to fill in themselves, you are using a **questionnaire**. Questionnaires need to be carefully planned and the questions you ask should be clear and simple.

Every person you survey should answer the same questions. People can answer the questions by checking boxes, marking a choice from a number of given ones or writing their own answers.

Here is an example of questionnaire used by a large hotel to see how satisfied guests are with the services.

Q4 How do you rate the following?	Very poor	Poor	OK	Good	Very good
Q4A Service	☐	☐	☐	☐	☐
Q4B Cleanliness	☐	☐	☐	☐	☐
Q4C Parking	☐	☐	☐	☐	☐
Q4D Quality of food	☐	☐	☐	☐	☐
Q4E Choice of food	☐	☐	☐	☐	☐

The data that you collect then needs to be organised to make it easy to read and work with. A **table** is useful for organising data. The table may have **tallies** and/or **frequencies**. This table combines tallies and frequencies to organise data from an interview of students in Level 5.

Maths ideas

In this unit you will:
* revise what you learnt last year about different methods of collecting data and what type of data suits each method
* collect your own data using observation, interviews and questionnaires
* use tallies and frequency tables to record and organise data.

Key words

collect data
survey
observation
interview
questionnaire
table
tallies
frequencies

Favourite place to read a book		
In bed	//// //// ////	15
Sitting on a chair	//// ////	9
Lying on the floor	//// ///	8
On the beach	//// //// //	12

1 Carry out a survey among your classmates to find out:
   a how many students wear glasses or contact lenses
   b what shoe size is most common in your class.

   Use tables like these to record and organise your data.

Wear glasses or contact lenses	Tally	Total

Shoe size	Tally	Frequency

2 Work in pairs.
   a Discuss how you would answer this questionnaire.
   b What do you think the designer of this questionnaire wanted to find out?
   c Is this a clear and simple questionnaire? Give reasons for your answers.

3 Work with a partner.
   a Design a questionnaire to find out what students in your year group do on Saturdays.
   b Swap your questionnaire with another pair. Assess each other's questionnaires and make suggestions for improvement.
   c Use your revised questionnaire to collect data from a different pair of students.

Name: _____ Date: _____

Please circle the correct information.

Sex: Male   Female

Age: 10–14   15–19   20–24

❶ Do you travel by public transport?   Yes No

❷ If yes, what sort of public transport do you use?
Bus   Sedan taxi   Mini-bus taxi   Tram   Train
Aeroplane   Ferry   Other: _____

❸ How much does your transport cost per week to the nearest dollar?
< $5 $6–$15 $16–$24
$25–$34 $35–$44   > $45

❹ If you were offered free public transport, what three things would you want to be part of the service you received:
1: _____
2: _____
3: _____

Thanks for your help with our survey.

4 Count the number of times each vowel appears in the verse. Record your results in a table like the one next to the verse.

All things bright and beautiful,
All creatures great and small,
All things wise and wonderful,
The Lord God made them all.

Vowel	Tally	Frequency
A		
E		
I		
O		
U		

5 Mrs Jones makes T-shirts to sell to tourists. She wants to find out what age groups visit her stall most often. She asks her son to do a survey of the visitors to her stall one morning while a cruise ship is docked in the harbour. Here are his results.

a Copy the table and complete it to organise the data.

Age group	Tally	Frequency
0–10		3
11–20	ЖЖ //	
21–30		12
31–40		32
41–50	ЖЖ ЖЖ ЖЖ ///	
51–60	ЖЖ ЖЖ ЖЖ	
>60	///	

b How does the table make the data easier to work with?

c How might this information be useful to Mrs Jones?

6 The number of persons whose inter-island flight was delayed by more than 30 minutes was recorded each day for 40 days at a local airport.

23 58 4 9 10 21 33 12 31 11 8 9 56 32 9 11 12 7 11 12
13 24 18 45 34 51 38 12 16 10 6 9 14 12 28 32 19 41 27 19

a Copy and complete this frequency table.

b Why do you think the number of passengers has been grouped in intervals of 10 for this data set?

c Who might find this data set useful? Why?

Number of passengers	Frequency
0–10	
11–20	
21–30	
31–40	
41–50	
51 or more	

What did you learn?

1 These survey questions all have something wrong with them. Discuss what is wrong and say how you would improve each one.

2 How would collect data to find out:

a how students get to school

b where most people buy their groceries

c which type of books students like to read

d how much time people spend on social media.

a How long do you spend studying each day? Please tick.

0–1 hours ☐   1–2 hours ☐   2–3 hours ☐   >3 hours ☐

b How much spending money do you get at the weekend?

None ☐   Not enough ☐   Enough ☐   Too much ☐

c Have you ever stolen something from a shop?

Yes ☐   No ☐

B Averages – the mean

Explain

An **average** is a figure that gives you a general picture of what a set of data shows. The average temperature for a month gives you an idea of more or less what you can expect that month. It does not tell you what the highest and lowest temperatures are – the actual temperature at any time during the month may be slightly higher or lower than the average.

The most commonly used average is the **mean**.

The mean of a set of data is the number you get when you add all the values in the set and then **divide** that **sum** by the number of values in the set.

Mean = sum of data values ÷ number of values in the set

Maths ideas

In this unit you will:
* calculate the mean of a set of data.

Key words

average

mean

divide

sum

> **Example 1**
>
> Find the mean of 5, 6, 8, 4 and 7.
>
> $5 + 6 + 8 + 4 + 7 = 30$
>
> $30 \div 5 = 6$
>
> **Example 2**
>
> Find the mean of 2, 7, 5, 4, 6 and 3.
>
> $2 + 7 + 5 + 4 + 6 + 3 = 27$
>
> $27 \div 6 = 4\frac{3}{6} = 4\frac{1}{2}$

You can see from the second example that the mean is not always a member of the data set, nor is it a whole number.

1 Find the mean of each set of data. Use a calculator if you have one.

    a 1, 1, 3, 4, 2, 2, 2, 4, 3, 3

    b 10, 20, 10, 15, 10, 11, 15, 15

    c 200, 200, 200, 200, 200

2 In his end-of-year exam, Stephen achieved these scores:

English	55%
History	34%
Geography	34%
Mathematics	90%
Science	87%

Calculate his year-end average.

3 The tables below show monthly rainfall data for Walt Disney World in Florida, USA, and Tokyo Disneyland in Japan.

Walt Disney World, USA: monthly rainfall in mm

Jan	Feb	Mar	Apr	May	Jun	Jul	Aug	Sep	Oct	Nov	Dec
59	71	77	51	76	175	208	211	162	66	43	55

Tokyo Disneyland, Japan: monthly rainfall in mm

Jan	Feb	Mar	Apr	May	Jun	Jul	Aug	Sep	Oct	Nov	Dec
50	72	106	129	144	176	136	149	216	194	96	54

a What is the mean monthly rainfall for the year in Tokyo Disneyland?

b What is the mean monthly rainfall for the year in Walt Disney World?

c Which park has the highest rainfall on average?

d What is the mean monthly rainfall from June to August for Walt Disney World?

e What is the mean monthly rainfall from June to August for Tokyo Disneyland?

f Which park is wetter from June to August?

Problem-solving

4 The total mass of 6 students is 387 kg. What is their mean mass?

5 Ten students recorded how many hours they spend on a computer each week. These were the results:

Class 5A: 16   23   21   5   12   0   5   13   14   11

Five students in Class 5B do the same thing. These are their results:

Class 5B: 9   11   4   16   15

a Find the average time spent on the computer each week for each class.

b Do the students in 5A or 5B spend more time on average on the computer?

c How would you work out an overall mean for both classes?

Investigate

6 Work in pairs. Choose any book.

a Investigate the average number of words in a line of text.

b Write a few sentences explaining how you worked out your answer.

c How would you estimate the average number of words per page?

What did you learn?

1 Calculate the mean of each data set.

a 120   124   123   180   140

b 12   13   12   14   16   12   18   20

2 A government says that the average family has $2\frac{1}{2}$ children. What does this mean?

Topic 8 Review

Key ideas and concepts

1   Copy this table and write short notes in each space to summarise what you know about collecting and organising data.

Method of collection	Steps of this method	Example of data that could be collected using this method
Observation		
Interview		
Questionnaire		

2   Write short notes to explain:

   a   how to record and organise data

   b   how to calculate the mean of a data set.

Think, talk, write …

1   Different people are interested in data for different reasons. Give an example of the data each of these people might need and suggest how they could collect and organise the data.

   a   A market stall vendor who sells T-shirts

   b   A tour company offering tours of your island

   c   A cricket coach in charge of selecting a team

   d   A ferry operator who wants to charge for trips to a small island

2   How can a very high or very low number in a set of data affect the average?

Quick check

1   A teacher is choosing caps for students to wear on a school trip. She wants to know which colour cap is the favourite among students in the class. There are 6 choices.

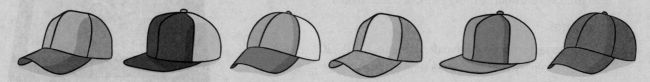

   a   Explain how you would carry out a survey to collect the data the teacher needs.

   b   Collect data from at least 20 students.

   c   Organise and record the data.

   d   Write a few sentences to summarise what you found out.

2   The number of fish caught at Rocky Point by different fishermen was recorded as 12, 16, 17, 3, 10 and 8.

   a   How do you think this data set was collected? Why was this method used?

   b   What is the average number of fish the fishermen caught?

Topic 9 — Number sense (3)

Teaching notes

Fractions

* Students have already learnt about unit fractions (with a numerator of 1, such as $\frac{1}{4}$), common fractions (such as $\frac{2}{3}$, $\frac{7}{8}$ and $\frac{9}{10}$), improper fractions (with a numerator greater than the denominator, such as $\frac{11}{7}$ or $\frac{9}{4}$) and mixed numbers (a combination of a whole number and a fraction, such as $1\frac{1}{2}$ and $3\frac{3}{4}$).
* This year, students will revisit equivalence and simplifying fractions. They will also convert between different forms of fractions. They will then use these skills to order and compare fractions.
* Students will use the work they have done on common multiples to find the lowest common denominator of a set of fractions to write them with the same denominator and compare them easily.

Decimals

* Although students may have come across decimal measurements and used decimal amounts of money, they are expected to deal with decimal place value formally in Level 5 for the first time.
* Many measurements in the metric system have a decimal point. For example, a bathroom scale may show that a person has a mass of 54.8 kilograms. The decimal point separates the whole kilograms (54) from the fraction part of a kilogram (.8 or 'point 8'). Point 8 is 8 tenths of a kilogram. You can write this as a decimal fraction (0.8) or as an ordinary fraction ($\frac{8}{10}$).
* Decimals (tenths and hundredths) can be indicated on the place value table by extending it to the right. Make sure students understand that everything to the right of the ones place is 'less than 1'.

Percentages

* A percentage is a fraction with a denominator of 100. It is written using a per cent symbol (%) rather than as a fraction, so $\frac{45}{100}$ would be written as 45%.

Ratio and proportion

* A ratio is a comparison of two or more quantities measured in the same units. Mixing quantities such as 1 cup water to 3 cups flour can be written as ratios (1 : 3). We read this as 1 : 3. This is not the same as $\frac{1}{3}$: 1 cup water plus 3 cups flour makes 4 cups, so the water is $\frac{1}{4}$ of the mixture!
* Proportion refers to a relationship between two quantities, for example, the price per litre of gas. The more gas you buy, the more you pay and the amount you pay increases in proportion (1 litre = 5 dollars, 2 litres = 10 dollars, and so on). The ratio between the number of litres and the price you pay remains the same, though: it is 1 : 5.

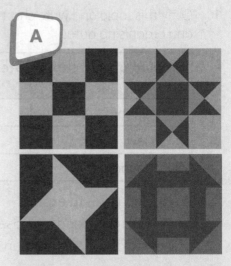

A

Mrs Ferguson is making a quilt by joining squares. These are some of the patterns she uses for the squares. Square one is $\frac{4}{9}$ green and $\frac{5}{9}$ purple. What fraction of a square is each colour on the other quilts?

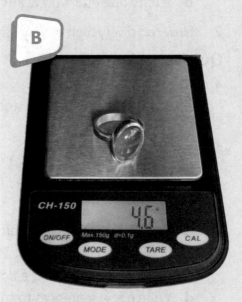

B

What is being measured here? What does the reading on the measuring instrument tell you? Why is there a dot between the numbers? What does the little g at the top right of the display tell you?

1234

C

Look at the numbers and symbols on this sign. What do you think these mean? Where else have you seen the % symbol used? What do you think it means in mathematics?

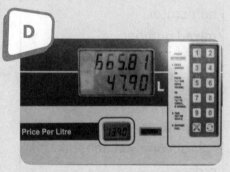

D

What information is given on a petrol pump display like this one? What is the price of petrol per litre shown here? What happens to the amount in the display as you pump more petrol into the car? Why?

Think, talk and write

A   Revisiting fractions (*pages 76–78*)

1   This square has been divided into four parts.

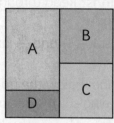

    a   Explain why each part is not $\frac{1}{4}$ of the square.

    b   How would you describe the different parts using fractions?

2   Which of these fractions are greater than $\frac{1}{2}$?

    $\frac{5}{10}$ $\frac{7}{8}$ $\frac{3}{4}$ $\frac{1}{4}$ $\frac{3}{7}$ $\frac{2}{3}$

B   Decimals (*pages 79–81*)

How would you write these money amounts using the decimal point?

1   Four dollars and twenty-five cents

2   Seventy dollars and fifty cents

3   Nine dollars and ninety-nine cents

4   Twelve dollars and sixty cents

C   Percentages (*pages 82–84*)

1   Carl read in his Social Studies book that 71 % of the Earth's surface is covered by the oceans, 3 % is covered by rivers and lakes and the rest is land.

    a   What do these figures mean?

    b   If $1\% = \frac{1}{100}$, what fraction of the Earth is land?

D   Ratio and proportion (*pages 85–86*)

1   1 kg of bananas costs $3.00.

    a   What is the cost of 4 kilograms?

    b   What is the relationship between the mass and the price?

2   This bottle of berry concentrate needs to be mixed with water in the ratio 1 : 3.

    a   Discuss what this means.

    b   If you use 2 capfuls of concentrate, how much water should you add? Why?

A Revisiting fractions

How much do you remember about **fractions**? Read through the information below to refresh your memory.

A fraction is a **part** of a **whole** object or a set. $\frac{1}{3}$, $\frac{17}{20}$ and $\frac{87}{100}$ are all fractions.

The **denominator** of a fraction is the number below the fraction bar. It tells you how many equal parts the whole is divided into.

The **numerator** is the top number in a fraction. It tells you how many parts of the whole you are dealing with.

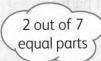

2 out of 7 equal parts

$\frac{2}{7}$ ←numerator→ $\frac{7}{11}$ ←denominator→

7 out of 11 equal parts

A **mixed number** is a combination of a whole number and a fraction. $1\frac{1}{2}$ and $4\frac{2}{5}$ are both mixed numbers.

$1\frac{1}{2}$ means you have one whole and half of the same sized whole.

Mixed numbers can be written as **improper fractions**. Improper fractions have a numerator that is greater than the denominator.

$1\frac{1}{2}$ means two halves (the whole) and another half ($\frac{1}{2}$).

This is $\frac{2}{2} + \frac{1}{2}$ which is $\frac{3}{2}$.

$\frac{7}{3}$ means seven thirds. This is $\frac{3}{3} + \frac{3}{3} + \frac{1}{3}$, which is the same as $2\frac{1}{3}$.

Equivalent fractions have the same value.

For example: $\frac{1}{2} = \frac{2}{4} = \frac{4}{8}$ and $\frac{3}{4} = \frac{6}{8} = \frac{30}{40}$

You can make equivalent fractions by multiplying or dividing the numerator and the denominator by the same number.

Example 1

$$\overset{\times 3}{\frac{3}{7} = \frac{9}{21}} \qquad \overset{\div 4}{\frac{8}{12} = \frac{2}{3}}$$
$$\underset{\times 3}{} \qquad \underset{\div 4}{}$$

A fraction is in its simplest form when it is as 'small' as possible. Mathematically, this means that the only factor that can divide into the numerator and denominator is 1.

$\frac{3}{4}$ is a fraction in its simplest form.

$\frac{9}{12}$ is not in its simplest form, because the 9 and the 12 can be divided by 3:

$\frac{9}{12} \div \frac{3}{3} = \frac{3}{4}$

You can **simplify** fractions in steps.

Example 2

$$\overset{\div 6}{\frac{18}{24} = \frac{3}{4}} \qquad \overset{\div 2 \ \div 2}{\frac{12}{16} = \frac{6}{8} = \frac{3}{4}}$$
$$\underset{\div 6}{} \qquad \underset{\div 2 \ \div 2}{}$$

This is not in its simplest form, so divide again.

In this unit you will:
* revise what you learnt in earlier levels about common fractions, improper fractions and mixed numbers
* convert fractions from one type to another
* generate equivalent fractions and simplify to give fractions in their lowest terms
* find a common denominator and use it to arrange fractions by size.

1   Look at the diagrams.

i   ii   iii   iv 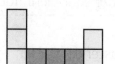 v   vi

a   What fraction of each of these diagrams is shaded yellow?

b   What fraction of each diagram is shaded green?

3   Write five fractions with a numerator of 3 and a value of one half or smaller.

4   How many different fractions can you make with the digits 1, 3, 5 and 9? List them.

5   Write each fraction in its simplest form.

a $\frac{2}{10}$ b $\frac{3}{12}$ c $\frac{6}{8}$ d $\frac{8}{10}$ e $\frac{9}{18}$ f $\frac{9}{27}$

g $\frac{7}{21}$ h $\frac{4}{12}$ i $\frac{15}{20}$ j $\frac{10}{2}$ k $\frac{16}{24}$ l $\frac{20}{100}$

6   Write these improper fractions as whole or mixed numbers.

a $\frac{12}{3}$ b $\frac{16}{3}$ c $\frac{19}{4}$ d $\frac{21}{7}$ e $\frac{13}{5}$ f $\frac{36}{6}$

g $\frac{100}{5}$ h $\frac{23}{5}$ i $\frac{18}{9}$ j $\frac{26}{6}$ k $\frac{100}{100}$ l $\frac{12}{9}$

7   Write each mixed number as an improper fraction.

a $2\frac{1}{2}$ b $4\frac{1}{3}$ c $2\frac{1}{4}$ d $3\frac{1}{8}$ e $6\frac{1}{2}$ f $2\frac{3}{4}$

Compare and order fractions

Explain

To **compare** fractions with the same denominator, look at the numerators.

$\frac{3}{8} < \frac{5}{8}$ $\frac{4}{9} > \frac{1}{9}$ $\frac{12}{40} < \frac{30}{40}$

If the denominators are different, find the **lowest common denominator** and make equivalent fractions.

Example 1

Compare $\frac{2}{3}$ and $\frac{2}{6}$.

Change $\frac{2}{3}$ to get sixths.

$\frac{2}{3} \times \frac{2}{2} = \frac{4}{6}$

$\frac{4}{6} > \frac{2}{6}$, so $\frac{2}{3} > \frac{2}{6}$

Example 2

Compare $\frac{2}{3}$ and $\frac{3}{5}$.

Change both fractions to get fifteenths.

$\frac{2}{3} \times \frac{5}{5} = \frac{10}{15}$ $\frac{3}{5} \times \frac{3}{3} = \frac{9}{15}$

$\frac{10}{15} > \frac{9}{15}$, so $\frac{2}{3} > \frac{3}{5}$

To **order** sets of fractions, make equivalent fractions with the same denominator.

Example

Arrange these fractions in ascending order: $\frac{5}{6}, \frac{1}{2}, \frac{1}{4}, \frac{2}{3}$

The lowest common multiple of the denominators is 12.

Change all the fractions to equivalent twelfths:

$$\frac{5}{6} \times \frac{2}{2} = \frac{10}{12} \qquad \frac{1}{2} \times \frac{6}{6} = \frac{6}{12} \qquad \frac{1}{4} \times \frac{3}{3} = \frac{3}{12} \qquad \frac{2}{3} \times \frac{4}{4} = \frac{8}{12}$$

The order is: $\frac{3}{12}, \frac{6}{12}, \frac{8}{12}, \frac{10}{12}$

Write the answer using the original fractions: $\frac{1}{4}, \frac{1}{2}, \frac{2}{3}, \frac{5}{6}$

8   Say whether these statements are true or false.

a $\frac{1}{2} > \frac{3}{5}$ b $\frac{6}{8} > \frac{4}{5}$ c $\frac{5}{6} = \frac{7}{8}$ d $\frac{1}{2} < \frac{4}{8}$

e $\frac{2}{3} < \frac{3}{9}$ f $\frac{9}{10} > \frac{2}{3}$ g $\frac{2}{5} < \frac{3}{8}$ h $\frac{2}{3} < \frac{3}{4}$

9   Compare each pair of fractions using the $<$ or $>$ signs.

a $\frac{2}{3}$ and $\frac{3}{4}$ b $\frac{6}{10}$ and $\frac{4}{5}$ c $\frac{1}{2}$ and $\frac{1}{3}$ d $\frac{1}{3}$ and $\frac{5}{12}$

e $\frac{2}{3}$ and $\frac{5}{6}$ f $\frac{4}{5}$ and $\frac{17}{20}$ g $\frac{2}{5}$ and $\frac{41}{100}$ h $\frac{1}{4}$ and $\frac{2}{5}$

10   Rewrite each set of fractions in ascending order.

a $\frac{1}{2}, \frac{3}{8}, \frac{1}{3}, \frac{1}{6}, \frac{1}{4}$ b $\frac{1}{2}, \frac{9}{10}, \frac{4}{5}, \frac{1}{10}$ c $\frac{3}{4}, \frac{7}{12}, \frac{1}{3}, \frac{5}{6}$

11   Rewrite each set of fractions in descending order.

a $\frac{2}{3}, \frac{1}{2}, \frac{5}{6}, \frac{7}{12}$ b $1\frac{3}{4}, 1\frac{4}{5}, 1\frac{6}{10}, 1\frac{1}{2}$ c $\frac{3}{4}, \frac{7}{10}, \frac{2}{5}, \frac{4}{5}$

12   $\frac{3}{4}$ and $\frac{6}{8}$ are equivalent fractions.

a   How could you show someone that even though the fractions are equivalent, they may not represent the same amount?

b   How many fractions equivalent to $\frac{3}{4}$ is it possible to make? Explain your answer.

What did you learn?

1   Look at the circle.

a   Write the fraction shown by each green sector.

b   Write an equivalent fraction for each one.

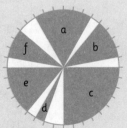

2   Compare these fractions using $<$, $=$ or $>$.

a $\frac{2}{8}$ and $\frac{1}{4}$ b $\frac{1}{5}$ and $\frac{2}{10}$ c $\frac{3}{4}$ and $\frac{7}{8}$ d $\frac{3}{4}$ and 1

B Decimals

Explain

Each of the big squares represents one whole. A fraction of each whole is shaded.

The shaded part of each square can be described as a common fraction or as an **equivalent** decimal using the **decimal point**.

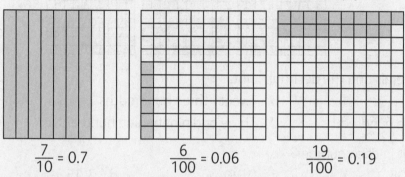

$$\frac{7}{10} = 0.7 \qquad \frac{6}{100} = 0.06 \qquad \frac{19}{100} = 0.19$$

The **digits** after the decimal point are called **decimal places**. The decimal 0.6 has one decimal place. The decimal 0.19 has two decimal places.

These decimals are both less than one, so they have to be written to the right of the ones column in the place value table. The place value table is extended to include **tenths** and **hundredths** like this.

Maths ideas

In this unit you will:
* extend the place value table to include tenths and hundredths
* work with decimal numbers that have up to two decimal places
* compare and order decimals
* convert between decimals and fractions.

Key words

equivalent	decimal places
decimal point	tenths
digit	hundredths

Hundreds	Tens	Ones	.		tenths	hundredths
		0	.		6	
		0	.		1	9

When the decimal fraction is less than 1 whole, you write a 0 before the decimal point (to show there are no ones).

Some decimal fractions contain whole numbers as well as fractional parts. The whole numbers are written before the decimal point (to the left of it).

Jonella is 1.39 metres tall.

You can show 1.39 on a diagram. Each large square represents one whole metre.

1 whole metre + $\frac{39}{100}$ parts of a metre

$1 + \frac{39}{100} = 1.39$ metres

You say 'one and thirty-nine hundredths of a metre' or 'one point three nine metres'.

You can also show 1.39 on a place value table.

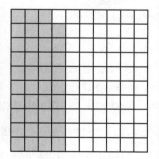

T	O	.	t	h
	1	.	3	9

Writing the decimal in expanded notation allows you to see the value of each digit.

1.39 = 1 + 0.3 + 0.09

1   Write the number shown in each diagram as a decimal.

a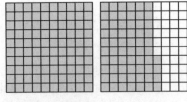

b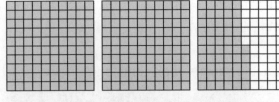

c

d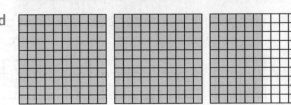

2   Write these numbers using numerals and the decimal point.
   a   Thirty-one and seven tenths
   b   Twenty-three hundredths
   c   One hundred twelve and nine hundredths
   d   Three and ninety-nine hundredths

3   What is the value of the red digit in each number?
   a   12.5**4**   b   3.**0**8   c   0.0**9**   d   3.4**5**
   e   1**0**0.98   f   10.0**7**   g   6**3**.25   h   9.9**9**

Problem-solving

4   Look at the digit 5 in each number: 47.5   5.13   0.35   3.56   50.6
   a   Which number has the highest value of 5?
   b   Which two numbers have the same value of 5?
   c   Which number contains 5 hundredths?
   d   How much is the 5 worth in 3.56?

5   The owner of a beach stall decides to
   increase her prices by $0.20. What will
   the new price of each of these items be?

$3.50 $4.25 $5.00 $6.75 $1.80

Compare and order decimals

Explain

You already know how to use place value to compare the size of whole numbers.
Remember these steps:
  ∗   Line up the places.   ∗   Work from left to right.
  ∗   Compare numbers digit by digit.   ∗   Find the first digit that is different.

You can use the same method to compare and order decimal fractions.
To do this, you must line up the numbers using the decimal point.
You can write 0 as a placeholder if that helps you.
Read through the example to see how this works.

Example

Order these lengths from longest to shortest:

231.3 m   14.802 m   99.09 m   14.81 m

Step 1:   Line up the decimal points.

Look at the whole numbers.
You can see 231 is the longest, then 99.

You do not need to compare the decimal places for these lengths.

H	T	O	.	t	h	th
2	3	1	.	3		
	1	4	.	8	0	2
	9	9	.	0	9	
	1	4	.	8	1	0

Look at the first place with different digits.

1 4 . 8 (0) 2
1 4 . 8 (1) 0

Compare these two next.

Step 2:

1 > 0

So 14.81 > 14.802

The answer is: 231.3 m, 99.09 m, 14.81 m, 14.802 m

6 Compare these numbers using <, = or >.
   a 3.4 and 3.04
   b 13.1 and 13.01
   c 0.28 and 0.82
   d 0.75 and 0.7
   e 0.49 and 0.45
   f 99.24 and 99.42

7 In the box you can see some of the 100 m sprint records set at the Olympics in the past 100 years. The times are recorded to a hundredth of a second.
   a Arrange the times from slowest to fastest.
   b What time is $\frac{3}{100}$ of a second faster than 9.58?

9.96	9.92	10.00
10.80	9.99	9.58

8 Write each set of measurements in order from greatest to smallest.
   a 2.04 km, 2.004 km, 2.104 km   b 0.131 ℓ, 0.031 ℓ, 0.13 ℓ   c 1.305 kg, 1.35 kg, 1.503 kg

9 Five gymnasts are taking part in a competition. The first four gymnast's scores are 9.8, 9.76, 9.79 and 9.82.
   a What is the lowest score the fifth gymnast needs if he wants to win?
   b If the fifth gymnast wins, which scores are second and third?

10 Mr James is building a machine. He needs a piece of metal that is between 1.4 m and 1.5 m long. He measures a piece and finds that it is 1.46 m long. Work out whether he can use it or not.

11 Convert these fractions to decimals.
   a $\frac{3}{10}$
   b $\frac{3}{100}$
   c $\frac{28}{100}$
   d $\frac{1}{2}$

What did you learn?

1 Write these money amounts in order from most to least.
   $9.00, $0.99, $9.90, $9.09, $0.09, $9.99

2 Write these numbers in ascending order: 0.72, 0.237, 0.7.

C Percentages

Per cent means 'for each hundred'. The symbol % is read as **per cent** and it shows that you are dealing with a **percentage**.

A percentage is really a fraction with a denominator of 100.

For example: seventy per cent is $\frac{70}{100}$ or 70%.

One hundred per cent (100%) is the whole.

(Remember that $\frac{100}{100}$ = 1.)

Look at the diagram carefully.

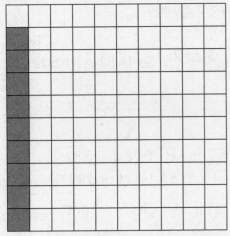

There are 100 small squares in the whole.

9 out of 100 small squares are shaded blue.

This can be written in three ways:

$\frac{9}{100}$ or 0.09 or 9%

These are different ways of writing the same value, so the values are **equivalent**.

$\frac{9}{100}$ = 0.09 = 9%

To **convert** a percentage to a decimal, write it as a fraction with a denominator of 100. Then convert the fraction to a decimal:

$85\% = \frac{85}{100} = 0.85$

Remember that a percentage is really a number of hundredths.

To convert a decimal to a percentage, write it as a fraction with a denominator of 100 and then as a percentage:

$0.72 = \frac{72}{100} = 72\%$

To write a fraction as a percentage, convert it to an equivalent fraction with a denominator of 100 and then to a percentage.

$\frac{2}{5} = \frac{2}{5} \times \frac{20}{20} = \frac{40}{100} = 40\%$

Maths ideas

In this unit you will:
* learn to understand the concept of per cent
* use diagrams and symbols to represent percentages
* understand how fractions decimals and percentages are related
* convert between fractions, decimals and percentages.

Key words

per cent

percentage

equivalent

convert

Important symbol

% means per cent

1 Write down five examples of where you would find percentages in daily life.

2 Julie has $100.00. She buys clothes for $47.00 and spends $10.00 on lunch.
a What percentage of her money has she spent?
b What percentage of her money does she have left?

3 What percentage of each shape is shaded yellow?

a
b
c
d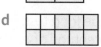
e
f
g
h
i

4 For each diagram, write the percentage represented by one part of the shape and the percentage of the shape shaded blue.

a
b
c
d
e

5 Convert each decimal to a percentage.
a 0.45
b 0.7
c 0.35
d 0.25
e 0.07
f 0.3
g 0.01
h 0.5
i 0.8
j 0.99

6 Convert each fraction to a percentage.
a $\frac{6}{10}$
b $\frac{9}{10}$
c $\frac{18}{100}$
d $\frac{8}{100}$
e $\frac{99}{100}$
f $\frac{1}{2}$
g $\frac{4}{5}$
h $\frac{9}{25}$
i $\frac{31}{50}$
j $\frac{5}{8}$

7 Write each percentage as an equivalent fraction and decimal.
a 89%
b 52%
c 6%
d 100%
e 4%
f 90%
g 30%
h 16%
i 25%
j $33\frac{1}{3}$%

8 A rectangle is divided into 5 equal parts. What percentage of the rectangle is:
a one part?
b three parts?
c five parts?

9   What percentage is left in each situation?

    a   Janae spent 15% of her pocket money on sweets and 32% on clothes.

    b   Leshawn spent 20% of his homework time on history and 34% on mathematics.

10   Anna scored $\frac{29}{40}$ in an English test and $\frac{17}{25}$ in a history test. In which subject did she get the highest percentage?

11   In Ms Walker's mathematics classes, 20 out of 100 students scored an A grade for a test. In Mr Darville's class, 4 out of every 20 students received an A grade. What percentage of each class scored an A grade?

12   Companies sometimes offer a percentage more food in a container at no extra cost. Look at the pictures and work out the mass of the special offer tin each case.

13   Garry keeps birds in an aviary. He has 27 green parrots, 15 ground doves and 8 red-necked pigeons.

    a   What percentage of the birds are parrots?

    b   What percentage of the birds are red-necked pigeons?

14   James gave $\frac{1}{5}$ of a cake to Sid and $\frac{2}{5}$ to Kim.

    a   What percentage of the cake did he give away?

    b   He eats half of what is left. What percentage of cake remains?

Challenge

15   Zayn has a piece of rope 3 m long. He cuts off 30% of the length. How many centimetres of rope did he cut off?

Investigate

16   Prepare a short presentation on percentages, fractions and decimals. Explain how percentages, fractions and decimals are equivalent. Use examples in your presentation.

    Look in newspapers and magazines for examples of percentages, fractions and decimals. Explain when it is more suitable to use a percentage, a fraction or a decimal.

What did you learn?

1   What do these mean?

    a   5 per cent   b   80 per cent   c   100%   d   200%

2   Write each percentage as a common fraction and a decimal.

    a   5%   b   10%   c   15%   d   100%   e   1%

D Ratio and proportion

Look at the counters. There are 4 red counters and there is 1 green one.

We can say that $\frac{4}{5}$ of the counters are red and $\frac{1}{5}$ of the counters are green.

A **ratio** is a way of comparing two quantities.

The ratio of red to green counters is 4 to 1. This means that for every four red counters there is one green counter.

We write this using the : symbol as 4 : 1.

We read it as '4 to 1'.

The order is important in a ratio:

* The ratio of red : green is 4 : 1, but the ratio of green to red is 1 : 4.

Fractions and ratios are not the same, so 1 : 3 and $\frac{1}{3}$ are not the same:

* In the fraction $\frac{1}{3}$, the denominator tells you the total number of **parts** (1) in the whole (3).
* In a ratio of 1 : 3, you have to add up the two numbers to get the total. So 1 : 3 means 1 out of a total of 4, which is the same as $\frac{1}{4}$.

Ratios do not have units. This is because the proportions are fixed, so the ratio works for any units:

* a ratio of 1 : 2 could mean 1 cup to 2 cups, 1 bag to 2 bags, 1 tonne to 2 tonnes or any other appropriate units.

You can reduce ratios to the lowest numbers to make **equivalent** ratios; for example:

* 9 : 3 can be reduced to 3 : 1 by dividing both numbers by 3.
* 25 : 5 can be reduced to 5 : 1 by diving both numbers by 5.

Maths ideas

In this unit you will:
* use ratios to compare numbers and amounts.

Key words

| ratio | equivalent |
| parts | compare |

Important symbols

: means 'to'
1 : 3 means 1 part to 3 parts

---

1   Write a ratio to **compare** each of these quantities.

a   red apples : green apples

b   bananas : mangoes

c   vanilla scoops : chocolate scoops

d   boys : girls

2   Read the words and then write down the ratio of vowels (a, e, i, o and u) to consonants in each word.

a   ratio   b   rectangle   c   parallelogram   d   mathematics

3   If there are two boys and three girls in a group of 5 students, we can say that $\frac{2}{5}$ of the group are boys.

a   What fraction are girls?

b   What is the ratio of boys to girls in this same group: 2 : 3 or 3 : 2 or 3 : 5? Why?

4   Look at these shapes.

A   B   C   D

   a   What fraction of each shape is green?
   b   What is the ratio of green parts to red parts in each shape?

5   Look at the results of a survey conducted among students in a class. Say whether each statement is true or false.

Morning drink	
Juice	Tea
13	6

   a   The total number of people surveyed was 19.
   b   6 out of 13 people drink tea in the morning.
   c   The ratio of people who drink tea to people who drink juice is 6 : 13.

6   Look at the fruit in this box.

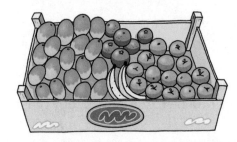

Write down these ratios in their simplest form.
   a   apples to oranges
   b   oranges to mangoes to apples
   c   bananas to mangoes
   d   mangoes to apples

Problem-solving

7   A painter wants to paint the walls of a room in pink. She mixes white and red paint in the ratio 4 : 1. She paints the wall, but the colour is too light. Which of these ratios should she use to get a brighter shade of pink: 1 : 5 or 3 : 1?

8   You need to cook enough rice to feed a crowd of 36 people. The instructions on the packet say you need one cup of rice to two cups of water to cook the rice successfully. The instructions also say that one cup of rice will feed four people. How many cups of water will you need?

What did you learn?

Look at the circle.

1   What fraction of the circle is orange?

2   What fraction of the circle is green?

3   Write the ratio of red to green parts.

4   Write the ratio of yellow to orange parts.

5   What colours are in the ratio 1 : 2?

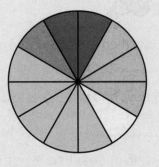

Topic 9 Review

Key ideas and concepts

Copy the mind map. Complete it to summarise the main things you learnt about each type of number.

Think, talk, write …

✳ List five examples of fractions or mixed numbers in everyday life.

✳ A friend asks you how to compare decimal fractions to decide which one is greater. What would you tell them?

✳ How are fractions, decimals and percentages similar? How are they different?

Quick check

1 What is the simplest form of each fraction?

   a $\dfrac{6}{10}$ b $\dfrac{16}{24}$ c $\dfrac{20}{25}$ d $\dfrac{15}{27}$ e $\dfrac{35}{100}$

2 Write a mixed number to answer these questions.

   a How many hours are 105 minutes?

   b How many metres are 125 centimetres?

   c How many years are 18 months?

3 Compare the fractions using the signs $<$, $=$ or $>$.

   a $\dfrac{5}{10}$ and $\dfrac{1}{2}$ b $\dfrac{1}{3}$ and $\dfrac{4}{10}$ c $\dfrac{1}{3}$ and $\dfrac{3}{10}$ d $\dfrac{4}{10}$ and $\dfrac{3}{12}$

4 What is the value of each of the digits in red?

   a 5 525.37   b 517.13   c 3.02   d 55.19   e 300.03

5 Write each fraction as an equivalent decimal and as a percentage.

   a $\dfrac{7}{10}$ b $\dfrac{32}{100}$ c $\dfrac{15}{20}$ d $\dfrac{9}{100}$ e $\dfrac{12}{25}$

6 Draw diagrams to show the following ratios of blue to yellow counters.

   a 1 : 3   b 2 : 1   c 2 : 5   d $\dfrac{1}{3}$ yellow

7 Can you solve these riddles? Write the answers.

   a I am a proper fraction. I am equivalent to $\dfrac{3}{5}$ but my denominator is 20.

   b I am a fraction equivalent to $\dfrac{3}{4}$. My denominator is greater than 16 but less than 21.

   c I am a mixed number between 2 and 3. The numerator and denominator of my fraction add up to 21. In simplest form it would be $\dfrac{3}{4}$.

Topic 10 Algebraic thinking

Teaching notes

Number sequences

* A sequence is a set of numbers that obeys a particular rule. For example, 2, 4, 6, 8, … is the sequence of even numbers, and 1, 4, 9, 16, 25, … is the sequence of square numbers.
* The numbers in a sequence can be in ascending or descending order.

Rules for number sequences

* Each number in a sequence is called a term.
* Number sequences can be generated from a rule. The rule tells you what to do to get the next term in a sequence. For example: Start at 0 and add 2 each time. This gives you the pattern of even numbers: 2, 4, 6, 8, …
* Tables are very useful for listing terms that help you work out the rule for a particular sequence.

Number sentences with unknowns

* Problems can be expressed in the form of number sentences with an unknown quantity, for example, $\boxed{} + 8 = 23$.

  The $\boxed{}$ in the number sentence represents the unknown value.
* Writing a number sentence with one or more unknown quantities is a useful problem-solving strategy. In Level 4, students worked with unknown quantities and showed them using empty boxes or other shapes. This year, students will use letters (such as x) to represent unknowns. The unknown letters are called variables in mathematics.
* Number sentences with an equals sign (=) are called equations. The quantities on either side of the sign must be equal. This means that if you perform an operation on one side of the equals sign, you must do the same operation on the other side to maintain the equality.

A

Look at this pattern. What will the next two shapes look like? Why? How many pegs are used to make each square? What types of numbers are these?

B

This thermometer shows the temperature on two different scales. Do you remember what they are called? When you know the temperature in degrees Celsius, you can use a mathematical rule to work out what the same temperature is in degrees Fahrenheit. The rule is $F = \frac{9}{5}°C + 32$. What do the F and C stand for in this rule? If the temperature is 30 °C, how would you use the rule to find the temperature in °F?

Think, talk and write

A **Number sequences** *(pages 90–91)*

1 These two number patterns each follow a different rule. Find the rule and work out the next three numbers in each pattern.
   a   13, 15, 17, 19, ___, ___, ___
   b   12, 24, 48, 96, ___, ___, ___

2 Look at this pattern.
   a   How many hexagons are there in the centre?
   b   How many yellow hexagons are in the first ring?
   c   How many orange hexagons are in the second ring?
   d   Work out how many hexagons you would need to build the next two rings.
   e   Where would you find a pattern like this in nature?

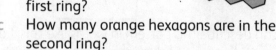

B **Unknown values and equations** *(pages 92–94)*

1 What do the following mean in mathematics?
   a   2 more than a number
   b   3 less than a number
   c   3 times as much as a number
   d   the product of a number and 4

2 How could you write the meanings in Question 1 using operation symbols? Share your ideas with your group.

3 Look at these two pattern machines. Work out the missing part of the rule and any missing numbers.

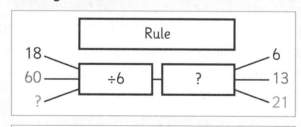

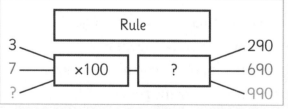

A Number sequences

A **number sequence** is a set of numbers that is arranged in a set order and according to a particular **rule**. The numbers in a sequence form a **pattern**. If you can see or work out the rule that was used to make the pattern, you can work out the value of other numbers in the sequence.

Look at this pattern made with rods.

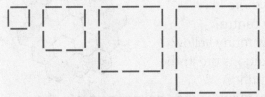

You can describe this pattern in words like this: Each shape in the pattern is a square. Each square is bigger than the one before it. The sides of the squares get longer each time. You add one more rod to the side each time.

Maths ideas

In this unit you will:
* work with sequences of numbers to find the rule used to make the sequence
* use the rule to find missing values in a sequence.

Key words

number sequence

rule

pattern

table

You can also describe the pattern using numbers. If you list the number of rods in order, you get a number sequence: 4, 8, 12, 16, …

You can see from the number sequence that each term is 4 more than the one before it. So, you can add 4 to find the next number: 16 + 4 = 20

Number sequences are useful for finding the next few numbers in a pattern, but sometimes you need to work out a number much further along the sequence. For example: How many rods will you need to build the 20th shape and the 100th shape in this pattern?

You can use a **table** to help you work this out.

Shape number	1	2	3	4	5	20	100
Number of rods	4	8	12	16			

The table helps you write a rule to work out how many rods you need to build any shape in the pattern.

The rule is   shape number × 4 = number of rods
So for the 5th shape: 5 × 4 = 20 rods
For the 20th shape: 20 × 4 = 80 rods
For the 100th shape: 100 × 4 = 400 rods

1   For each pattern on the next page:
   * draw the next two shapes
   * write the pattern as a number sequence
   * write a rule for the pattern.

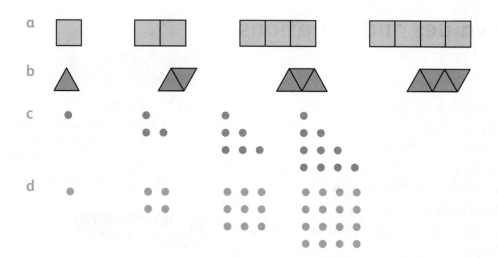

a
b
c
d

2   For each number sequence, work out the rule used to generate it and write the next three terms.
    a   10, 20, 30, 40, ...   b   30, 60, 90, 120, 150, ...   c   10, 100, 1 000, ...

3   A class is looking at this dot pattern. The teacher asks the students to work out how many dots will be needed for the 10th shape.

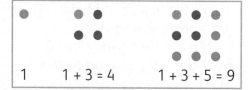

1   1 + 3 = 4   1 + 3 + 5 = 9

Janine says this pattern is made by adding odd numbers. For the first shape, you add one odd number, for the second you add the first two odd numbers and for the third you add the first three odd numbers. So, to find the number of dots in the tenth shape she would add the first ten odd numbers.

Maria says there is an easier way to work out the answer because these are square numbers. What does Maria mean?

4   Make up a shape pattern of your own. Exchange patterns with a partner. Try to find the rule your partner used and use it to draw the next two shapes in the pattern.

Problem-solving

5   Michael builds towers using dominoes like this:
    a   Without drawing or building the houses, work out how many dominoes Michael needs to build each of the next five houses.
    b   List the sequence for the number of dominoes needed for each house. Compare these numbers with the sequence of square numbers. What do you notice?

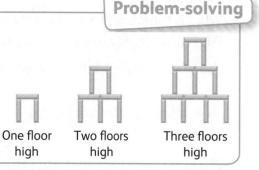

One floor high   Two floors high   Three floors high

What did you learn?

1   Look at this pattern.
    What will the next shape look like? Why?

2   What are the next three numbers in each sequence?
    a   2, 4, 6, 8, 10, ...
    b   27, 24, 21, 18, 15, ...
    c   6, 11, 16, 21, 26, ...

B Unknown values and equations

Explain

In mathematics, we often have to **solve** problems involving **unknown** amounts. For example: If the sum of two different whole numbers is 11, what could the numbers be?

In this example, you do not know what the numbers are, but you do know that if you add them together you get 11.

Previously, you may have written this as ☐ + ◯ = 11

The different shapes in the **number sentence** show that the two numbers are different.

In mathematics, you can use letters instead of empty shapes for unknown numbers.

So, you could write this problem as $a + b = 11$.

In this example, a and b stand for different numbers, but the value of a and b can vary.

* If a is 1, then b must be 10.
* If a is 2, then b must be 9.

Because the value can change (or vary), we call these letters **variables**.

The number sentence $a + b = 11$ is called an **equation**.

Any number sentence with an equals sign is an equation.

The equals sign in an equation is very important. It tells you that both sides of the number sentence have the same value. It also means that you can change the equation as long as you change the parts on either side of the equals sign the same way.

Maths ideas

In this unit you will:
* write number sentences to represent word problems
* solve number sentences to find the unknown values.

Key words

solve	variables
unknown	equation
number	inverse
sentence	

Example

What is the value of x if $14 + x = 20$?

(You can probably see the answer right away, but follow the working anyway.)

You want to know what x is, so you have to get it on its own.

To do that, you can subtract 14.

$$14 + x = 20$$
$$\downarrow \qquad \downarrow$$
$$\text{Subtract 14} \qquad \text{Subtract 14}$$
$$x = 6$$

If you subtract 14 from the left-hand side, you need to subtract 14 from the right-hand side as well to keep the two sides equivalent.

You can also use **inverse** operations to find the missing values.

Remember: if $2 + 6 = 8$, then $8 - 6 = 2$, so if $x + 6 = 8$, then $8 - 6 = x$.

$$14 + x = 20$$
$$x \longrightarrow \boxed{+14} \longrightarrow 20$$
$$x \longleftarrow \boxed{-14} \longleftarrow 20$$
$$\text{so} \quad x = 6$$

You can check your answers by putting the number you have found in place of the variable and making sure the number sentence is true.

$6 + 14 = 20$, so $x = 6$ is correct.

1   Solve these equations.

    a $3 + x = 7$ b $2 + y = 9$

    c $2 + y = 10$ d $1 + x = 50$

    e $14 - x = 4$ f $5 - x = 1$

    g $x + 12 = 23$ h $y + 15 = 50$

    i $y + 1\frac{1}{2} = 3$ j $3 \times x = 27$

    k $x \times 9 = 54$ l $8 \times y = 24$

    m $12 \div x = 4$ n $x \div 4 = 20$

    o $35 \div y = 7$

2   Find the value of the variable in each equation.

    a $a \times 4 = 48$ b $x + 34 = 82$

    c $32 - x = 12$ d $x \div 2 = 20$

    e $20 - a = 5$ f $m \times 8 = 40$

    g $25 = s + 3$ h $15 \times m = 165$

3   Work out the value of x in each of these equations. Remember to apply the order of operations rules wherever there is more than one operation.

    a $2x + 11 = 25$

    b $(x + 10) \times 5 = 500$

    c $5 \times x - 100 = 150$

    d $x \times 10 - 12 = 48$

    e $3 \times x - 15 = 12$

    f $x \times 2 + 14 = 30$

Problem-solving

4   Write an equation to represent each problem. Then solve the equation to work out the unknown value.

    a 5 more than x is 14

    b 10 more than y is 200

    c 3 less than a is 121

    d 45 minus b is 0

    e half of x is 32

    f twice y is 50

5   Find all the possible values of m and n in these equations.

    a $160 \div 20 = m \times n$

    b $32 - 17 = m + n$

    c $100 - 40 = m \times n$

    d $32 + 48 = 2 \times m + n$

6   Look at this puzzle and its solution. Each letter represents a single-digit
    number. If the letter appears more than once, it has the same value each time it appears.

FORTY	29 786
TEN	850
+ TEN	850
SIXTY	31 486

Here are some examples. Try to find a set of numbers that works for each one.

a
```
    A
    B
 + AB
 ___
   BA
```

b
```
  CCC
 + D
 ____
 DEEE
```

c
```
    M
    M
 + M
 ___
   LM
```

Now try these. Find at least two different number solutions for each calculation.

d
```
   NINE
 − FOUR
 _____
   FIVE
```

e
```
  THREE
 + FOUR
 _____
  SEVEN
```

What did you learn?

1   What number does n represent in each of these number sentences?
    a $4 + n = 20$
    b $4 \times n = 20$
    c $n \div 4 = 20$
    d $20 \div n = 2$
    e $n - 8 = 7$

How did you work out the answers?

2   Write an equation for each statement and solve it.
    a   11 plus y is equal to 20.
    b   7 less than x is 4.
    c   The difference between 11 and m is 9 (m is greater than 11).
    d   The product of 8 and n is 32.
    e   Twice m is 4 more than 20.

Topic 10 Review

Key ideas and concepts

Match each word on the left to its correct meaning on the right.

sequence	the product of a number and itself
rule	instruction for generating a pattern
variable	an ordered set of numbers that follow a pattern
equation	a calculation written with numbers and an equals sign
square number	a letter used to represent unknown numbers
solve	count in groups

Think, talk, write …

Where can you find these patterns in your environment?

1   A pattern of odd and even numbers

2   A pattern made of repeating rectangular shapes

3   A pattern made of triangles

Quick check

1   Describe each sequence. Write down the next three numbers in each one.

   a   1, 4, 7, 10, _____, _____, _____

   b   101, 99, 96, 92, _____, _____, _____

   c   2 916, 972, 324, _____, _____, _____

2   Look at this pattern.

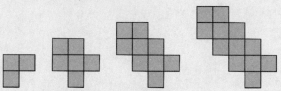

   a   Describe in words how it works.

   b   How many squares will you need to make the next shape?

   c   Write a number sequence to match the pattern.

   d   Work out how many squares you would need for the 20th shape in this pattern. Show how you do this.

3   Write each of these as a mathematical equation and find the value of n.

   a   The sum of n and 4 is 13.
       b   The sum of n and 9 is 17.

   c n less 7 results in 12.
       d   The product of n and 8 is 56.

   e   The sum of twice n and 3 is 21.

4   An equilateral triangle has a perimeter of x. What is the length of each side?

5   Nadia says 'I am thinking of a number. When it is multiplied by 3 and the product is increased by 5, the result is 17'. What number is she thinking of?

Topic 11 Measurement (2)

Teaching notes

Perimeter

* Perimeter is a measure of the total length of the boundaries (sides) of a shape.
* You can measure perimeter, but you can also calculate perimeter if you are given the lengths of the sides.
* To calculate perimeter, you find the sum of the lengths of all sides of the shape.

Area

* The area of a flat shape is the amount of space it covers.
* Area is measured in squares. Students have already counted squares to work out the area of different shapes.
* Standard units of area are called square units. A square with sides of 1 cm makes 1 square centimetre (1 cm²).
* Larger areas can be measured in square metres or square kilometres.
* The area of many shapes can be calculated using a formula. For example, the area of a rectangle with length 4 cm and width 2 cm can be calculated using the formula
area = length × width
so: 4 cm × 2 cm = 8 cm²

Real-life applications

* Many real-life problems involve calculating perimeter and area.
* The project in this topic shows how both concepts are used to plan and build a coop for keeping chickens.
* The project will help prepare students for assessment projects and equip them with skills they can apply in their own lives.

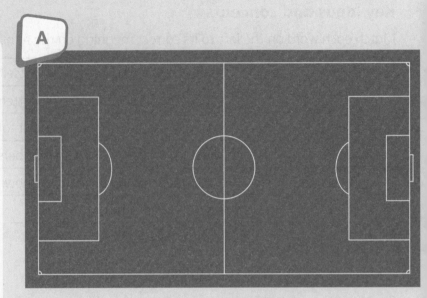

A

This is a bird's-eye view of a football field. What shapes can you see on the field? The white lines are painted with a special paint using a small machine. How would you work out how far the machine travels to paint all the lines? What units would you use?

C

Mrs Nestor wants to install a new light switch like this one, but she is not sure what size to get. When she removes the old light switch, she finds an area of wall that is damaged. She wants the new cover to hide this. How would she check whether the new cover will be big enough to hide the damaged area before she buys it?

B

Which piece of paper has the same surface area as the front cover of the exercise book? Which piece of paper is smaller than the book? Which piece of paper could you use to cover the book?

A   Perimeter *(pages 98–99)*

1   If you wanted to buy a door to fit in your classroom, what would you have to measure?

2   Draw rough sketches to show three different rectangles that all have a perimeter of 16 cm. Write the lengths of the sides on your sketches.

B   Area *(pages 100–101)*

1   Work in pairs. Cut out a square piece of paper that is 10 cm long and 10 cm wide. This is one square unit.

   Investigate how many square units you would need to cover the surface of:

   *   your desk
   *   the whiteboard or blackboard
   *   the window in your classroom.

2   Compare your answers with another pair. Tell each other how you worked them out.

C   Perimeter and area in real life *(page 102)*

1   Where do people need to measure and use perimeter in their daily lives? List as many examples as you can.

2   How would the following people use area in their jobs?

   a   A tiler
   b   A fashion designer
   c   A painter
   d   A doctor
   e   A farmer

A Perimeter

The **perimeter** of a flat shape is the **distance** around it.

To measure the perimeter of a shape, you need to **measure** the **length** of each **side** and then add the lengths together. So you find the **sum** of the sides.

If the lengths of the sides (dimensions) are given, you don't need to measure, you just add them together to **calculate** the perimeter.

When you work with diagrams, you may have to use the properties of shapes to work out lengths which are not given.

Maths ideas

In this unit you will:
* understand that perimeter is the sum of the lengths of the sides of a shape
* measure and calculate the perimeter of shapes
* make up and solve problems involving perimeter.

Example

What is the perimeter of this rectangle?

Find the missing measurements first.

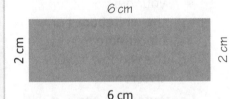

This is a rectangle, so the opposite sides are the same length.

Perimeter = 2 cm + 6 cm + 2 cm + 6 cm = 16 cm

Key words

perimeter	side
distance	sum
measure	calculate
length	

Think and talk

The distance round the outside of a circle is not called the perimeter. Do you remember what it is called?

1   Measure the perimeter of each shape in centimetres.

a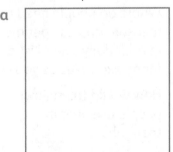

b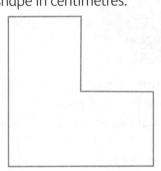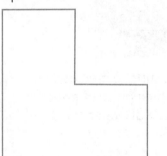

c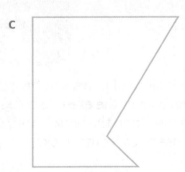

2   Calculate the perimeter of each shape.

a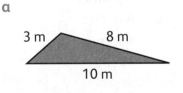

b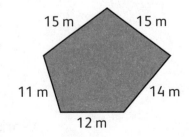

c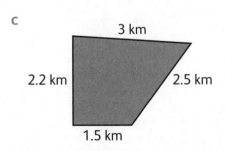

3   Calculate the perimeter of each rectangle.

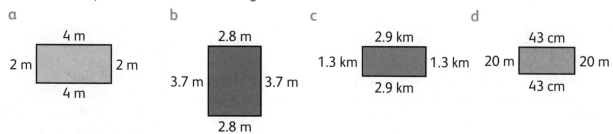

a   b   c   d
4 m   2.8 m   2.9 km   43 cm
2 m   2 m   1.3 km   1.3 km   20 m   20 m
4 m   3.7 m   3.7 m   2.9 km   43 cm
                   2.8 m

4   Look at your work from Question 3.

    a   Can you find a short cut for calculating the perimeter of a rectangle?

    b   A square has four equal sides. Can you find a short cut for calculating the perimeter of
        a square?

Problem-solving

5   Work out these perimeters.

    a   A square photograph with each side 20 cm long

    b   A pillowcase with a length of 60 cm and width of 45 cm

    c   A rectangular mirror with length 2.4 m and height 0.5 m

6   Solve these problems.

    a   A poster board has a length of 90 cm and a width of 65 cm. Julia needs enough tape to
        make a border all the way along the edge of the poster. Calculate the perimeter of the
        board to work out how much tape she needs.

    b   Alicia makes a square cake with each side 24 cm long. What length of ribbon would she
        need to go around the cake?

    c   A photograph is 16 cm wide by 8 cm long. James calculates the perimeter after adding
        an extra half centimetre on each end of each side to work out how much tape he needs
        to stick the photograph in his album. What is the total length of the tape?

    d   The perimeter of a square tile is 160 cm. What is the length of each side?

    e   A rectangle has one side of 11 cm and a perimeter of 38 cm. What are the lengths of the
        other three sides? Make a rough sketch and write in the lengths.

Challenge

7   How many different rectangles can you draw with a perimeter of 60 cm?

What did you learn?

1   Write your own definition of perimeter.

2   Calculate the perimeter of each item.

    a   A photo with height of 21.5 cm and width of 18.5 cm

    b   A square sticker with all sides equal to 24 mm

    c   A birthday card with height of 155 mm and width of 87 mm

B Area

You already know that you can work out the **area** covered by a shape by counting how many **square units** are inside the shape.

Shape A has an area of 8 squares.

Shape B has an area of 9 squares.

Shape A is bigger in area than Shape B because the squares are bigger.

To work with area and to compare the area of different shapes we need to use a standard unit. Square units depend on the **length** of the side of the square.

This square has sides that are 1 cm long.

This is a one centimetre square.

We write one centimetre square in short form like this: 1 cm².

We use square millimetres and **square centimetres (cm²)** for small areas and **square metres (m²)** and **square kilometres (km²)** for larger areas.

You can calculate the number of square units in a rectangle without counting them.

Look at rectangle A again.

Maths ideas

In this unit you will:
* revise what you learnt about area in earlier levels
* learn about square units of measurement
* calculate area in square units
* develop a formula for working out the area of a rectangle
* solve problems involving irregular areas.

Key words

area
square units
length
square centimetres (cm²)
square metres (m²)
square kilometres (km²)
width (breadth)
formula

Rectangle A is 4 units long and 2 units wide. If you count the square units you get 8 squares.

If you multiply 4 × 2, you also get 8 squares.

Try this with shape B and you will get the same result. In shape B the length and **width** are equal. (Width is sometimes also called **breadth**.)

This gives us a rule or **formula** for finding the area of any rectangle: area = length × width

The unit of the answer depends on the units in the problem.

If the side lengths are centimetres, the answer will be in centimetres squared (cm²).

If the side lengths are in metres, the answer will be in metres squared (m²).

1   Count the number of square units in each shape to find the area. Check that you get the same answer using the formula.

a

b

c

100

2   Sally put some plastic rectangles onto a sheet of one-centimetre squared paper. Use the formula to find the area of each rectangle. If you get stuck, you can draw them on squared paper and count the squares to check your work.

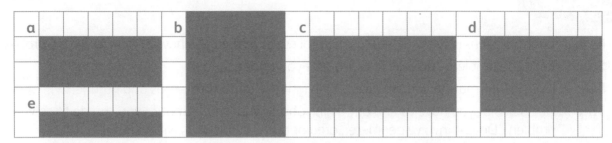

3   a   Calculate the area of each rectangle below.

     b   How can you calculate the area of the green shaded triangles?

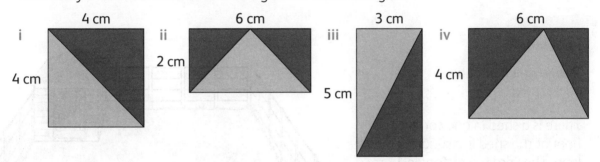

Problem-solving

4   Find the length and width of a rectangle that has an area of 100 square centimetres and a perimeter of 50 centimetres.

5   Use the formula for area (area = length × width) to give the length and width of as many different rectangles as you can with an area of 48 centimetres squared.

6   A rectangular vegetable plot is 8 m long. It has an area of 40 square metres. The farmer increases the length of the plot by 2 m. He wants the new plot to have an area of 60 square metres. By how much does he need to increase the width?

7   Shawnae has 18 metres of rope. She wants to mark out a rectangle with the greatest possible area using the rope. The sides of the rectangle must be whole number lengths. Work out the length and width of the rectangle she should make.

What did you learn?

1   Which one of the following units is NOT used for calculating area:

     cm²   km²   cm   mm²

2   What is the difference between perimeter and area?

3   A rectangular field has a length of 35 m and a width of 22 m.

     a   What is its perimeter?

     b   What is its area?

C Perimeter and area in real life

Read through the steps in the problem-solving process to remind you how to work to solve a problem.

Step 1: Read the problem carefully to make sure you understand it.

Step 2: List the information you are given. Highlight the important words and numbers.

Step 3: Decide what you have to find out. Think about what mathematics you can do to solve the problem. Does it involve perimeter, area or both? What units will you use?

Step 4: Choose a strategy. When the problems involve shape and space, it is often useful to draw diagrams and to make rough sketches to work out what you need to do.

Project

Plan a chicken coop

This is Mr Richardson's back yard.

There is a shed in one corner. The floor of the shed is a square 2 metres long. The yard is a rectangle 12 m long and 7 metres wide. The rest of the yard is covered in grass.

1   Use a sheet of squared paper. Let the sides of the squares on the sheet represent 50 cm in reality.

    a   Draw a plan of the yard and show the shed on the plan.

    b   Calculate the area covered by grass.

2   Mr Richardson wants to build a coop for keeping his chickens. He wants it to be as big as possible, but 2 metres around the outside of the coop should remain open.

    a   Use your plan of the yard to decide where Mr Richardson should build the enclosure. Sketch it on the plan.

    b   He wants to fence the enclosure and install a gate that is 80 cm wide. Work out the length of fencing he will need to enclose the coop.

3   Each chicken needs an area of at least 50 centimetres squared. Work out the total area of the coop and calculate how many chickens it can hold.

4   Mr Richardson has to decide whether to use gravel or to pave the walkway that is 2 m wide around the coop. The gravel costs $145.00 for 200 kilograms. He will need 6 kilograms per square metre. The paving costs $24.50 per square metre and it will cost another $50.00 to have it laid. Which should he choose if he wants the cheaper option?

Topic 11 Review

Key ideas and concepts

Which words are missing from these statements about perimeter and area?

1   Perimeter is the _____ around a shape.

2   You can calculate the perimeter by _____ the lengths of each _____ of a figure.

3   The _____ of a circle is the distance around the circle or its perimeter.

4   Area is the amount of space a flat figure takes up, measured in _____.

5   To calculate the area of a rectangle you can use the _____ A = length × width.

Think, talk, write ...

1   Look at this scarf and read the measurements.

   a   Which measurement is the perimeter of the scarf?

   b   Which measurement is the area of the scarf?

   c   What is the difference between perimeter and area?

   d   How do you calculate each measurement?

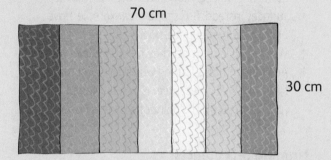

70 cm

30 cm

Measurement A: 200 cm   Measurement B: 2 100 cm²

2   Make up three problems about perimeter and area and give them to your partner to solve.

Quick check

1   These shapes were drawn on one-centimetre squared paper. What is the perimeter and area of each shape?

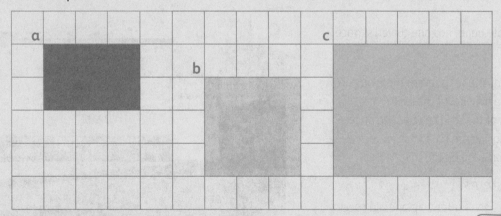

Problem-solving

2   An athlete runs twice around a rectangular field that measures 96 m by 70 m. How far does she run altogether?

3   Jeffrey wants to cover a square with glass. What area of glass will be needed if the table is 45 cm long?

4   The cost of cleaning a carpet is $8.50 per square metre. How much will it cost to clean a rectangular carpet that is 3 metres wide and 4 metres long?

Teaching notes

3-D objects and their parts

* Solid objects are three-dimensional (3-D) objects because they have three dimensions that you can measure: length, breadth and height.
* Flat surfaces on 3-D objects are called faces.
* Some 3-D objects don't have faces but curved surfaces instead. Ball shapes, for example, have only one curved surface, no faces.
* Where two faces meet they form an edge.
* Any corner that is formed where three (or more) faces of a 3-D object meet is called a vertex (plural: vertices). The point of a cone is also called its vertex.

Naming 3-D objects

* Solids are named according to the number and shape of their faces.
* A cube has six square faces.
* A cuboid or rectangular prism has six rectangular faces (some may be square).
* A cone has a flat circular base and a curved surface that forms a point (the vertex).
* A cylinder has two flat circular end faces and a curved surface.
* A sphere (or ball shape) has one curved surface.

Nets

* A net is the template (or pattern) that you can fold up to make a model of the solid.
* All of the faces of the solid can be seen on the net and the fold lines on the net show where faces meet at an edge on the solid.

Coordinate systems

* In mathematics, the Cartesian plane is a special grid with an *x*-axis and a *y*-axis that is used to plot points and draw graphs.
* The position of any point on the grid can be given using two coordinates. These are given as a pair and the *x*-coordinate is always first (x, y).
* To find the position of a given point, locate the numbers on the *x*-axis and *y*-axis and move up and across to the point where they meet.

A

Why are these beads three-dimensional objects? What criteria have been used to put them into groups? Can you name the groups? Which group doesn't have a mathematical name? Why? What shape do all the beads have in common?

C

GPS systems like this one can be programmed with coordinates that are used to find places. The position of every place on the Earth can be given using a set of coordinates. For example, Castries is located at coordinates 14 N 61 W. Discuss how coordinates work and how they can help you find places.

B

Mrs Joyson saw coloured boxes like the one above on a website and ordered some for her craft business. When they arrived in the post, they looked like the one at the bottom. What does Mrs Joyson have to do to get the boxes to look like the one above?

Think, talk and write

A   3-D objects *(pages 106–108)*

1   Sketch an example of each of these 3-D objects.
   a   A short fat cylinder
   b   A cube
   c   A short wide cuboid
   d   A cone

2   Where would you find examples of each type of object in real life?

B   Nets of 3-D objects *(pages 109–110)*

Mr Rasmus wants to make wooden boxes like this one to sell at the market. Draw all the pieces of wood he will need to make each box.

C   Coordinates on a grid *(page 111–112)*

Look at this seating plan of an aeroplane.

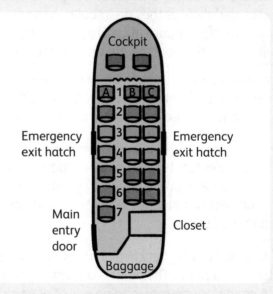

1   How are the seats numbered?

2   Sandra is flying to Grenada. Her ticket says her seat number is 5B. Where is her seat?

3   Her friend is two rows behind her at the window. What is her seat number?

A 3-D objects

Solid objects are three-dimensional because they have length, width and height.

Cubes, cuboids, cones, cylinders and spheres are all 3-D.

3-D objects have faces, edges and vertices.

* A **face** is a **flat** side of a solid.
* An **edge** is where two faces of a solid meet.
* A **vertex** is a point where three or more faces of a solid meet.

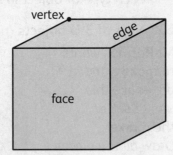

Read this information to revise the properties of different solids. Make sure you know the name of each one and that you know its properties.

Maths ideas

In this unit you will:
* revise the mathematical names of parts of shapes
* use the properties of different 3-D shapes to identify and name them.

Key words

face	cylinder
flat	circular
edge	curved
vertex	cone
cube	apex
vertices	sphere
cuboid	

A **cube** is a solid object with six square faces. All the surfaces are flat, so there are twelve edges and eight **vertices**. Cubes make very good six-sided dice, as they are regular in shape and each face is the same size. In the diagram of a cube, three of the faces are labelled, all the lines are edges and all the vertices are marked with a dot.	face, face, face
A **cuboid** is box shape with six rectangular faces. Like a cube, a cuboid has six faces, eight vertices and twelve edges. Mathematically, a cube is a square-faced cuboid. Remember that a square is a special type of rectangle.	face, face, face
A **cylinder** has two flat **circular** faces, and one **curved** surface. Since the two faces do not meet, a cylinder has no edges and no vertices. Examples of cylindrical objects include canned food tins, batteries and glue sticks.	face
A **cone** has one flat circular face (its base), and a curved surface that ends in a point. The point is a special type of vertex called an **apex**. A cone has one face, and no edges or vertices. A traffic cone, an ice-cream cone and a party hat are examples of cones.	base
A **sphere** is a round three-dimensional object. Since a sphere has only a curved surface and no flat surface, it has no faces, edges or vertices. Balls, oranges and marbles are examples of spheres.	

1   Here are some examples of 3-D objects found in the real world.
    a   Name the objects shown.
    b   List at least five more examples of these objects in the real world.

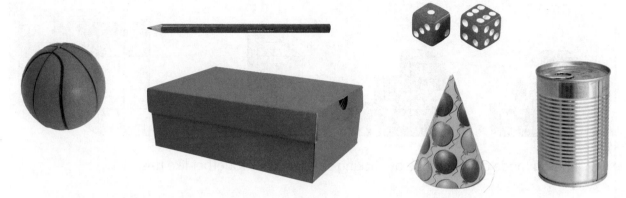

2   Draw and name each 3-D object from the clues given.
    a   This box has only rectangular faces.
    b   This tube has two circular end faces, but no vertices.
    c   This object has square faces and eight vertices.
    d   This object can roll, but it has no faces or edges.
    e   This object has a flat base and the curved surface ends in a point.

3   Read these statements carefully. Write the names of all the 3-D objects for which the statement is true.
    a   Each edge is perpendicular (at right angles) to four other edges.
    b   There are no perpendicular edges.
    c   There are no vertices.
    d   There are six edges.
    e   There are opposite faces that are parallel.
    f   All the faces are square.
    g   There are no edges.

4   A group of students started to draw some 3-D objects. What object (or objects) do you think each person was drawing? Explain your answer.

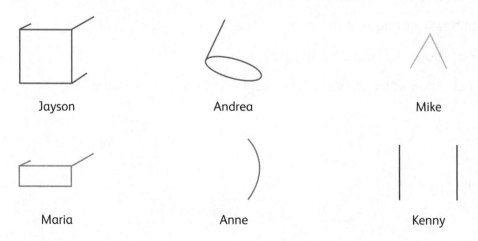

Jayson   Andrea   Mike

Maria   Anne   Kenny

5   These objects have been built using cubes. Assume they are solid throughout
    and work out how many cubes were used to build each solid.

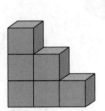 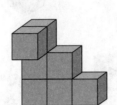 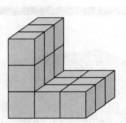 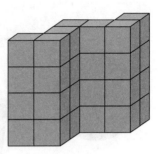

6   Sharon made a model cube by sticking smaller cubes together like this.

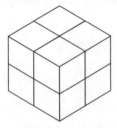

Her brother knocked the model over and it broke into three parts. Which of these could be the
three parts? Explain why the other two could not be the three parts.

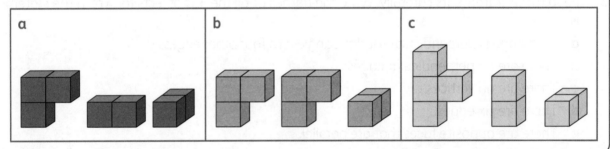

a	b	c

What did you learn?

1   Why does a sphere not have any edges or vertices?

2   Why does a cone not have any edges or vertices?

3   Why does a cylinder not have any edges or vertices?

4   Why does a cuboid have the same number of faces, edges and vertices as a cube?

B Nets of 3-D objects

A **net** is a flat pattern that can be folded up to make a 3-D object.

If you unfold a box you can see the shapes of the faces and the **fold lines** where the edges meet.

These are both nets of the same cuboid. The matching faces are the same colour on each diagram. The coloured lines show the edges that join together.

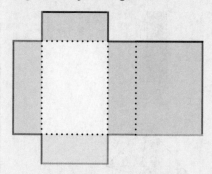

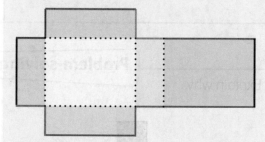

If you **cut out** the nets and fold along the dotted lines you can make model cuboids as shown below.

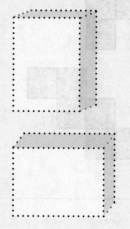

Maths ideas

In this unit you will:
* revisit nets of 3-D objects
* use nets to make 3-D models.

Key words

net
fold line
cut out

1   Match the nets in column A to the object they would make if you folded them up in column B.

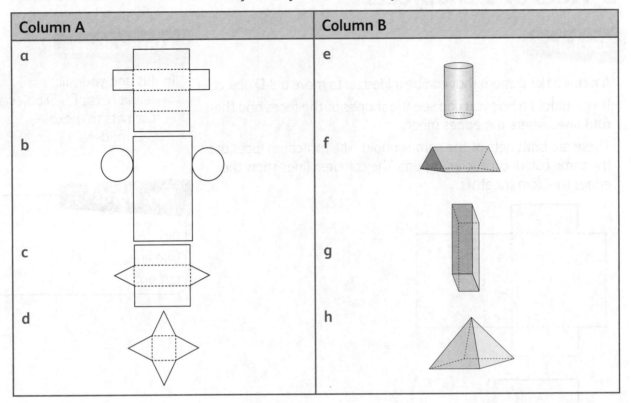

Column A	Column B
a	e
b	f
c	g
d	h

Problem-solving

2   Which of these nets can be folded up to make a cube? Explain why some of them do not work.

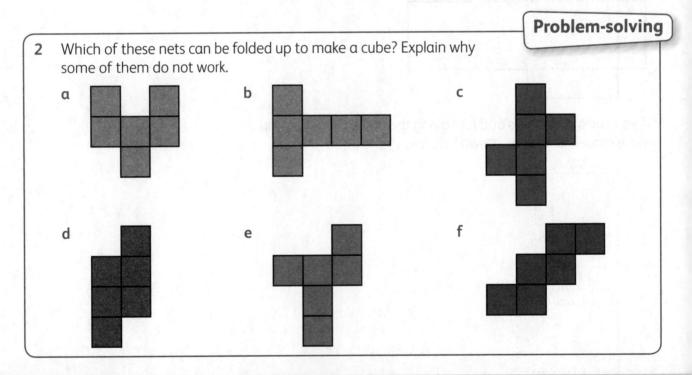

What did you learn?

1   Find a box at home. Open it up to see its net and sketch it.

2   Sketch a net that you could use to make an open-topped cube-shaped box. Use colours to show which edges would match up.

C Coordinates on a grid

Explain

The **grid** shows the **position** of different places at a marine park.

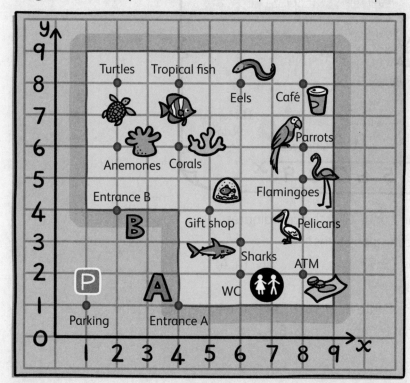

Maths ideas

In this unit you will:
* learn how to use coordinates and a grid to give positions
* plot points on a grid and use coordinates to find points on a grid.

Key words

grid

position

coordinates

axes

x-axis

y-axis

origin

Each position on the grid can be described using a pair of numbers. For example, Entrance A is at position 4 across and 1 up.

The numbers are the **coordinates** of the position and they are written as a pair in brackets, like this: (4, 1).

The grid is drawn with two **axes**. An **x-axis** goes across horizontally (remember that X is a cross) and the **y-axis** goes up vertically. The point where the axes meet is called the **origin**. Its coordinates are (0, 0).

The order of the coordinates is important. We always read the number from the *x*-axis first (remember that X comes before Y in the alphabet).

The toilets (WC) are at position (6, 2).

The anemone display is at position (2, 6).

1   Look at the map of the marine park again. What is found at each of these coordinates?
   a (1, 1)   **b** (2, 8)   **c** (8, 2)   **d** (8, 8)

2   What are the coordinates for each of these places at the marine park?
   a Entrance B   **b** the eels   **c** the parrots   **d** the gift shop

3   Suggest two positions that would be good to place exit gates. Give a reason for your choice.

4   A new display of lionfish is to be placed halfway between the corals and the parrots. What are the coordinates of the new display?

5   The map shows the route that a helicopter flies on a tour around an island.

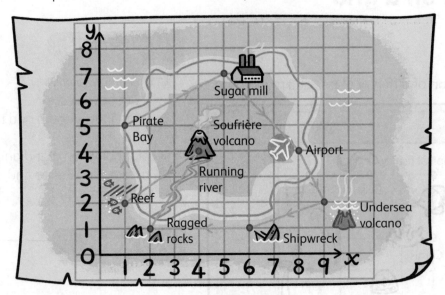

a   Where does the flight start and end? Give the coordinates.

b   What can you see at the following positions?

    i   (6, 1)   ii   (5, 7)   iii   (4, 4)

c   What are the coordinates of:

    i   the reef?   ii   Pirate Bay?   iii   the undersea volcano?

d   Where is the helicopter when it is at position (3, 6)?

What did you learn?

This grid shows the position of various places on an island.

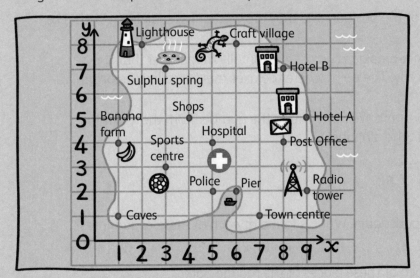

Work with a partner.

Make up ten questions about positions on the grid. Write them on a sheet of paper.

Write the answers to your questions on a separate sheet.

Exchange questions with another pair and answer theirs. Check each other's answers.

Topic 12 Review

Key ideas and concepts

Answer these questions to summarise what you learnt in this topic.

1   What properties do cubes and cuboids share?

2   What is the difference between a cylinder and a cone?

3   What is a net and how do you make one?

4   How does a coordinate system work?

Think, talk, write ...

1   Four students started to build models of a cube using smaller blocks. What is the fewest number of blocks each person will need to complete their cube? Assume that you can see all the cubes they have used so far and that no cubes are hidden.

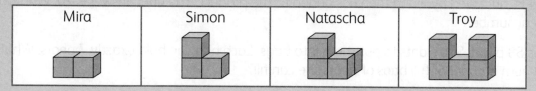

Mira	Simon	Natascha	Troy

2   What is the difference between the coordinates (3, 4) and (4, 3)?

Quick check

1   What shape do you get if you glue two cubes together? Why?

2   Mrs Harding wants to line a large rectangular tank with plastic. The tank looks like this:

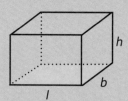

She has one sheet of plastic and only four lengths of waterproof tape. Explain, with drawings, how she could line the tank.

3   Look at the grid.

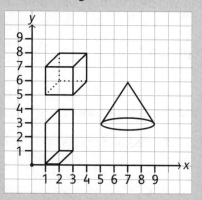

a   Where is the origin on this grid and what are its coordinates?

b   Write the coordinates of each vertex of the cube.

c   What is found at point (7, 6)?

Test yourself (2)

Explain

Complete this test to check that you have understood and can manage the work covered in
Topics 1 to 12.
Revise any sections that you find difficult.

1   Read the table. What is David's score?

Name	David	Jimmy	Sharon	Total
Score	?	824	718	2 341

2   A number is multiplied by 2 and then 6 is added to the product. The final answer is 20. What was
the original number?

3   Maria has 58 pears. She wants to put them into bags. Each bag can hold exactly 7 pears. What is
the maximum number of full bags of pears she can fill?

4   Write four thousand and seventy-five dollars in numbers.

5   This table shows the revenue a banana farmer earned from banana sales over four months.

February	March	April	May
$53 987	$76 432	$64 300	$72 154

a   During which month did the farmer earn the greatest revenue?
b   During which month did the farmer earn the least revenue?
c   Write the total sales for April in words.
d   Round the revenue for May to the nearest hundred dollars.

6   Write 40 as a product of its prime factors.

7   Determine the highest common factor of 8, 12 and 16.

8   John wanted to measure the diameter of a 10¢ coin. Which unit will be the most appropriate to
use: millimetres, metres or kilometres?

9   On a map, 1 cm represents 20 km. What distance does 5 cm represent?

10   Express 5 metres in centimetres.

11   Tom ran 650 cm, Peter ran 9.5 m and Ezra ran 75 m. Who ran the shortest distance?

12   One book weighs 248 grams. One bag weighs 338 grams. What is the mass of 3 books and the bag?

13   Which diagram best represents an obtuse angle?

a    b   c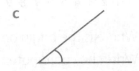

14 The amount a container can hold when it is full is called its _____.

15 At birth a baby weighed 3 000 g. What is that in kilograms?

16 Arrange the fractions $\frac{5}{7}, \frac{5}{6}, \frac{5}{9}$ in order from smallest to greatest.

17 Maria has these fruits:

bananas   cherries   soursop   apples

What fraction of the fruits are the bananas?

18 Write $3\frac{8}{9}$ as an improper fraction.

19 Which one of these statements is true?

a $\frac{2}{6} = \frac{1}{3}$ b $\frac{2}{6} < \frac{1}{3}$ c $\frac{2}{6} > \frac{1}{3}$

20 Write an equivalent fraction for $\frac{3}{5}$.

21 Reduce $\frac{12}{18}$ to its simplest form.

22 What is the value of the 3 in 1.53?

23 Write the numeral for two and three hundredths.

24 Write a fraction that represents the number of sections shaded. Then express each fraction as a decimal and a percentage.

a   b   c

25 There is an 8 % sales tax in Food Fair. For each dollar spent, how much money do you pay as sales tax?

26 a What is the perimeter of this shape in centimetres?

    b What is the area of the shape? Show how you worked this out.

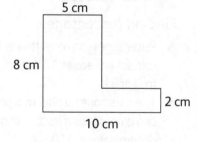

31 Refer to the table and name shapes A, B and C.

Shape	Faces	Vertices	Edges
A	6	8	12
B	3	0	2
C	1	0	0

33 John wants to find out how many students in his class arrive at school on time on the first day of the new school year. What is the best method he can use to obtain that data?

34 You were asked to conduct a survey to find out how people feel about a new sandwich shop coming to their community. How would you collect the data? Give reasons for the method you choose.

Teaching notes

Adding and subtracting fractions

* Students already know how to add and subtract fractions with the same denominators and they have learnt to make equivalent fractions.
* When you work with fractions with different denominators, you use equivalence to find the lowest common denominator. This is simply the lowest common multiple of the denominators.
* Mixed numbers are easier to work with if you convert them to improper fractions first. Then they are treated like any other fraction you add or subtract.

Multiplying and dividing fractions

* To multiply a whole number by a fraction, you write it as a fraction with a denominator of 1 ($5 = \frac{5}{1}$, for example). Then you can multiply numerators by numerators and denominators by denominators. This is the same principle as when you multiply a fraction by any other fraction.
* When you divide a fraction by a whole number, such as $\frac{1}{2} \div 6$, you are really finding $\frac{1}{6}$ of the half. $\frac{1}{6}$ of a half means $\frac{1}{6} \times \frac{1}{2}$. This is why you invert the fraction you are dividing by ($\frac{6}{1}$ becomes $\frac{1}{6}$) and then multiply.

Calculating with decimals

* Place value is important when working with decimals. Students need to line up decimal places and insert decimal points in products. Decimal calculations are otherwise done in the same way as whole number calculations.

Finding percentages

* Percentages can be written as fractions or decimals to make calculations easier. 12 % of 30 is $\frac{12}{100} \times \frac{30}{1} = \frac{360}{100}$, which is equivalent to $\frac{36}{10}$ or $3\frac{3}{5}$.
* To express one number as a percentage of another, you write the two amounts as a fraction and find the equivalent fraction with a denominator of 100.

Profit and loss

* Profit or loss is the difference between what you pay for an item (the cost) and what you sell it for. Actual profit or loss can be worked out by adding or subtracting decimals, and the answer is a money amount.
* Percentage profit or loss can be calculated using the formula $\frac{\text{profit}}{\text{cost price}} \times 100$ or $\frac{\text{loss}}{\text{cost price}} \times 100$. This is the same calculation as expressing one number as a percentage of another.

A

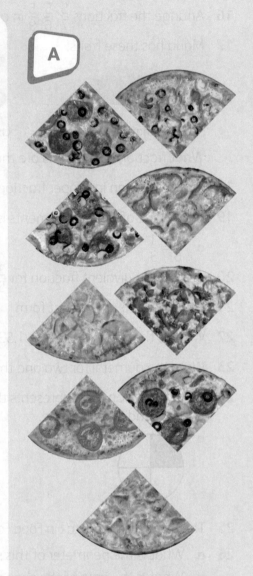

What fraction of a whole pizza is each of these slices? How much pizza is here? Give your answer as a mixed number and as an improper fraction. If 4 of these slices were eaten, how much would be left? Sharyn takes one slice and divides it equally among three friends. What fraction of a pizza do they each get? Carrie eats $\frac{1}{2}$ of a slice, what fraction of a pizza is this?

1234

This is the route of a trail run. What is the total length of the route? How far from the start is the halfway mark? A runner trains for the race by running the route three times a week. How far does she run each week? There are three first aid stations equally spaced along the route. How far apart are they?

C

$400

Mr Khan sells office furniture. He has to raise his prices by 15% because the cost of materials has increased. What will the new price of this item be? Tell your partner how you worked this out.

Think, talk and write

A Calculate with fractions *(pages 118–121)*

1 The diagram shows $2\frac{1}{3}$.
   a How many thirds is that in all?
   b What is $2\frac{1}{3} - 1\frac{2}{3}$?

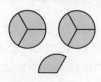

2 Nisha had $18.00. She gave each of her two brothers $\frac{1}{6}$ of the money and her sister $\frac{1}{3}$ of the money.
   a What fraction of the money did she give away?
   b What fraction did she have left?
   c How much money did she have left?

B Calculate with decimals *(pages 122–125)*

1 Mr Bantam buys five items at the airport. The prices are given below.

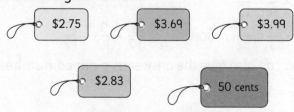

$2.75 $3.69 $3.99

$2.83   50 cents

   a How much change would he get from $20.00?
   b How would you solve this problem?
   c Try your method. Compare your answers with a partner's.

2 A metre of fabric costs $36.50. What is the cost of:
   a 10 metres?   b 12 metres?

3 Sammy paid $122.00 for 4 metres of fabric. What was the cost per metre?

C Calculate with percentages *(pages 126–128)*

1 Use percentages to work out which is greater in each pair. Show your partner your workings.
   a 21 out of 30 or 70 out of 100
   b 40 out of 160 or 30 out of 150

2 Sarah bought some shoes for $80 but they didn't fit her very well. She sold them to a friend for $60.
   a How much money did she lose on the sale?
   b Express her loss as a percentage.

A Calculate with fractions

Explain

To add or subtract fractions with the same denominators, you add or subtract the numerators and write the answer with the same denominator.

$$\frac{6}{8} + \frac{1}{8} = \frac{7}{8} \qquad \frac{7}{10} - \frac{3}{10} = \frac{4}{10}$$

If the denominators are different, you can make **equivalent fractions** that have the same denominator. It is most efficient if you use the **lowest common denominator (LCD)**: the LCD is the number that is the **lowest common multiple (LCM)** of the denominators.

Example 1

$\frac{2}{3} + \frac{3}{4}$ The LCM of 3 and 4 is 12.

$$\frac{2}{3} \times \frac{4}{4} = \frac{8}{12}$$

$$\frac{3}{4} \times \frac{3}{3} = \frac{9}{12} \quad \text{So,} \ \frac{2}{3} + \frac{3}{4} = \frac{8}{12} + \frac{9}{12} = \frac{17}{12}$$

You can also give the answer as a **mixed number**:

$$\frac{17}{12} = 1\frac{5}{12}$$

Example 2

$\frac{2}{5} - \frac{1}{4}$ The LCM of 4 and 5 is 20.

$$\frac{2}{5} \times \frac{4}{4} = \frac{8}{20}$$

$$\frac{1}{4} \times \frac{5}{5} = \frac{5}{20} \quad \text{So,} \ \frac{2}{5} - \frac{1}{4} = \frac{8}{20} - \frac{5}{20} = \frac{3}{20}$$

Example 3

To add or subtract mixed numbers, convert them to improper fractions and then write them with the same denominators.

$$3\frac{1}{2} - 1\frac{3}{4}$$

$$3\frac{1}{2} = 1 + 1 + 1 + \frac{1}{2} = \frac{2}{2} + \frac{2}{2} + \frac{2}{2} + \frac{1}{2} = \frac{7}{2}$$

$$1\frac{3}{4} = \frac{4}{4} + \frac{3}{4} = \frac{7}{4}$$

The LCM of 2 and 4 is 4. $\frac{7}{2} = \frac{14}{4}$

So, $3\frac{1}{2} - 1\frac{3}{4} = \frac{14}{4} - \frac{7}{4} = \frac{7}{4} = 1\frac{3}{4}$

Maths ideas

In this unit you will:
* add, subtract, multiply and divide fractions
* solve problems involving different kinds of fractions.

Key words

equivalent fractions

lowest common denominator (LCD)

lowest common multiple (LCM)

mixed number

simplify

inverse

cancel

Key skill

Check that you remember how to multiply or divide to find equivalent fractions and **simplify** fractions, for example:

$$\frac{3}{5} \times \frac{4}{4} = \frac{12}{20}$$

$$\frac{9}{12} \div \frac{3}{3} = \frac{3}{4}$$

1 Find the LCD of each pair of denominators. Write the equivalent fractions.

a $\frac{4}{5}$ and $\frac{3}{4}$ b $\frac{5}{6}$ and $\frac{1}{8}$ c $\frac{2}{7}$ and $\frac{3}{2}$ d $\frac{2}{4}$ and $\frac{1}{5}$

e $\frac{2}{3}$ and $\frac{3}{5}$ f $\frac{1}{6}$ and $\frac{3}{7}$ g $\frac{1}{2}$ and $\frac{8}{9}$ h $\frac{4}{5}$ and $\frac{5}{7}$

2 Try to do these calculations mentally. Give the answers in simplest form.

a $\frac{7}{8} - \frac{4}{8}$ b $\frac{3}{4} - \frac{1}{4}$ c $\frac{5}{6} - \frac{4}{5}$ d $\frac{9}{7} - \frac{3}{7}$

e $1\frac{3}{5} - \frac{3}{5}$ f $2\frac{1}{3} + 3\frac{1}{3}$ g $4\frac{3}{10} + \frac{2}{10}$ h $1\frac{9}{10} + \frac{1}{10}$

3 Use equivalent fractions to find the answers to each calculation.

a $\frac{4}{5} + \frac{2}{3}$ b $\frac{7}{4} + \frac{4}{3}$ c $\frac{12}{7} - \frac{13}{14}$ d $\frac{1}{2} - \frac{2}{5}$

e $\frac{3}{10} + \frac{4}{5}$ f $\frac{7}{3} + \frac{3}{2}$ g $\frac{2}{6} + \frac{3}{9}$ h $\frac{8}{3} - \frac{5}{6}$

i $\frac{1}{4} + \frac{1}{2}$ j $\frac{2}{7} + \frac{3}{21}$ k $\frac{2}{3} + \frac{2}{15}$ l $\frac{1}{9} + \frac{1}{18}$

m $\frac{5}{6} - \frac{4}{12}$ n $\frac{15}{10} - \frac{12}{40}$ o $\frac{3}{4} - \frac{2}{3}$ p $\frac{7}{8} - \frac{3}{4}$

Problem-solving

4 What is the perimeter of a rectangle $2\frac{3}{5}$ m wide and $3\frac{1}{10}$ m long?

5 One day (24 hours) in the holidays, Marshall spent $\frac{1}{3}$ of the day asleep, $\frac{1}{6}$ of the day eating, $\frac{1}{12}$ of the day doing chores and $\frac{3}{8}$ of the day playing computer games. What fraction of the day is left?

6 In the grounds of a hotel, $\frac{1}{3}$ of the area is occupied by the swimming pool and $\frac{1}{5}$ of the area is occupied by the dance floor. $\frac{1}{10}$ is used for pathways. What fraction of the area is left over?

7 Jean makes fruit punch for her beach stall. This is her recipe.

a How much does the recipe make altogether?

b Jean makes the punch in a bucket with a capacity of 10 litres. She adds water to the mixture to fill the bucket. How much water should she add?

> $1\frac{3}{4}$ litres of orange juice
>
> $1\frac{3}{4}$ litres of lime juice
>
> $4\frac{1}{2}$ litres of lemonade

Challenge

8 Three students have picked cards with fractions on them. Read what they say and work out what fraction each student has.

Maria: My card has a fraction that is one half greater than one third.

Sandra: Mine is a fraction in simplest form. It is a quarter less than five eighths.

Royston: My fraction has an odd numerator and a denominator of 5. If you subtract half from it, you'll end up with $\frac{1}{10}$.

Explain

Last year you multiplied fractions by whole numbers.

Read through these examples to remind you how to do this.

Example 1

What is $4 \times \frac{1}{5}$?

$4 \times \frac{1}{5} = \frac{4}{1} \times \frac{1}{5} = 4 \times \frac{1}{1} \times 5 = \frac{4}{5}$

Example 2

What is $\frac{3}{10}$ of 40?   In mathematics, the word 'of' means that you have to multiply.

$\frac{3}{10} \times \frac{40}{1} = 3 \times \frac{40}{10} \times 1 = \frac{120}{10} = 12$

Example 3

You can use the same methods to multiply fractions by other fractions.

What is $\frac{3}{4}$ of $\frac{1}{2}$?

$\frac{3}{4} \times \frac{1}{2} = 3 \times \frac{1}{4} \times 2 = \frac{3}{8}$

Look at the diagram to check that this is correct.

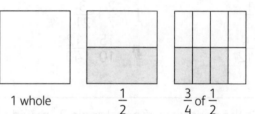

1 whole $\frac{1}{2}$ $\frac{3}{4}$ of $\frac{1}{2}$

This is $\frac{3}{8}$ of the whole.

Example 4

You can divide fractions into smaller pieces, for example:

$\frac{1}{2} \div 5$

Look at the diagram.

Can you see that dividing something (the half) into 5 equal parts is the same as finding $\frac{1}{5}$ of it?

$\frac{1}{5}$ of $\frac{1}{2} = \frac{1}{5} \times \frac{1}{2} = 1 \times \frac{1}{5} \times 2 = \frac{1}{10}$

Each piece is $\frac{1}{10}$ of the whole.

$\frac{1}{5}$ of $\frac{1}{2}$ is $\frac{1}{10}$

$\frac{1}{2} \div 5$

This gives us a method for dividing fractions using multiplication.

$\frac{3}{4} \div 8$ Think: we need $\frac{1}{8}$ of $\frac{3}{4}$.

$\frac{3}{4} \div \frac{8}{1}$ Write the whole number as a fraction.

$\frac{3}{4} \times \frac{1}{8}$ Use the **inverse** of the fraction and multiply.

$= \frac{3 \times 1}{4 \times 8} = \frac{3}{24}$

In this example, you need to simplify the answer.

$\frac{3}{24} \div \frac{3}{3} = \frac{1}{8}$

9 Calculate.

a $\dfrac{1}{2} \times \dfrac{3}{4}$ b $\dfrac{3}{4} \times \dfrac{5}{6}$ c $\dfrac{7}{8} \times \dfrac{7}{8}$ d $\dfrac{3}{5} \times \dfrac{2}{3}$

e $\dfrac{2}{3}$ of $\dfrac{1}{6}$ f $\dfrac{5}{6}$ of $\dfrac{3}{10}$ g $\dfrac{5}{8}$ of $\dfrac{1}{6}$ h $\dfrac{5}{6}$ of $\dfrac{5}{8}$

10 Multiply. Simplify (**cancel**) before you multiply where possible.

a $\dfrac{8}{9} \times \dfrac{3}{5}$ b $\dfrac{7}{10} \times \dfrac{5}{8}$ c $\dfrac{1}{3} \times \dfrac{9}{20}$ d $\dfrac{1}{2} \times \dfrac{4}{5}$

e $\dfrac{1}{2} \times \dfrac{8}{10}$ f $\dfrac{3}{10} \times \dfrac{5}{6}$ g $\dfrac{5}{8} \times \dfrac{2}{10}$ h $\dfrac{2}{3} \times \dfrac{3}{4}$

i $3 \times \dfrac{5}{6}$ j $\dfrac{11}{12} \times 4$ k $\dfrac{3}{5} \times \dfrac{10}{13}$ l $\dfrac{7}{10} \times \dfrac{5}{21}$

11 Find the product.

a $\dfrac{3}{4} \times \dfrac{9}{10}$ b $\dfrac{15}{20} \times \dfrac{3}{4}$ c $\dfrac{18}{25} \times \dfrac{3}{4}$ d $\dfrac{3}{10} \times \dfrac{15}{16}$

e $\dfrac{49}{100} \times \dfrac{3}{7}$ f $1\dfrac{1}{3} \times \dfrac{3}{4}$ g $\dfrac{2}{3} \times 12$ h $\dfrac{3}{4} \times 2\dfrac{1}{2}$

12 Apply the correct order of operations rules to do these mixed calculations.

a $\dfrac{1}{2} \times \dfrac{3}{5} - \dfrac{1}{4}$ b $\left(\dfrac{3}{8} + \dfrac{1}{3}\right) \times \dfrac{3}{10}$ c $\dfrac{1}{4} \times \dfrac{2}{3} + \dfrac{2}{3}$

d $\dfrac{1}{3} \times \dfrac{1}{4} + \dfrac{3}{8}$ e $\dfrac{5}{9} - \dfrac{3}{10} \times \dfrac{5}{6}$ f $\dfrac{3}{5} + \dfrac{7}{10} - \dfrac{1}{2} \times \dfrac{4}{15}$

g $\dfrac{14}{15} \times \dfrac{5}{7} + \dfrac{4}{5}$ h $\left(\dfrac{2}{3} + \dfrac{5}{6}\right) \times \dfrac{1}{2}$ i $\dfrac{3}{4} - \dfrac{2}{5} \times \dfrac{1}{2}$

13 Divide.

a $\dfrac{1}{4} \div 2$ b $\dfrac{4}{5} \div 12$ c $\dfrac{2}{3} \div 6$ d $12 \div \dfrac{1}{4}$

e $15 \div \dfrac{1}{5}$ f $4 \div \dfrac{2}{3}$ g $\dfrac{1}{4} \div 2$ h $\dfrac{1}{2} \div 10$

Problem-solving

14 Darren has to walk $\dfrac{9}{10}$ of a kilometre to school. He is $\dfrac{1}{3}$ of the way there. How much further does he have to walk?

15 Mr Benson has 1 740 mangoes to sell. He has sold $\dfrac{5}{12}$ of them. How many has he sold?

16 $\dfrac{4}{5}$ of 320 students walk to school. How many do not walk?

17 What is the area of a rectangular flower bed that is $\dfrac{3}{5}$ m wide and $\dfrac{7}{8}$ m long?

18 $\dfrac{3}{4}$ of a loaf must be shared equally among 5 persons. What fraction of the loaf will each one get?

19 Shireen has 2 kg of rice. She puts it into smaller bags, each holding $\dfrac{1}{8}$ of a kilogram. How many bags can she fill?

20 Anna has 2 litres of juice. How many glasses can she fill if each glass holds $\dfrac{3}{10}$ of a litre?

What did you learn?

Calculate.

1 $\dfrac{3}{4} + \dfrac{2}{9}$ **2** $\dfrac{7}{8} - \dfrac{1}{3}$ **3** $\dfrac{1}{3} \times 2\dfrac{1}{7}$ **4** $\dfrac{3}{10} \div 6$

B Calculate with decimals

Decimals can be added and subtracted in **columns** using place value in the same way as whole numbers.

When you write decimals in columns to add or subtract them, you must line up the **decimal point** in the calculation and the answer.

You can fill empty places with **placeholders** (0) to make it easier to add or subtract in columns.

Maths ideas

In this unit you will:
* use the methods you already know to add and subtract decimals in columns
* explore short methods for multiplying decimals by 10, 100 and 1 000
* multiply decimals by whole numbers.

Key words

decimals

columns

decimal point

placeholders

regroup

digits

factors

decimal places

Example 1

What is the sum of 0.4 + 2.3 + 5.17?

$$\begin{array}{r} 0.40 \\ 2.30 \\ + \ 5.17 \\ \hline 7.87 \end{array}$$

0.40   Write the decimals in columns. Line up the decimal points.

2.30   Fill in 0 as a placeholder in empty places.

+ 5.17   Add as you would add whole numbers.

7.87   Write the decimal point in the answer.

Example 2

Add 2.07 + 14.59.

2.07   Write the decimals in columns. Line up the decimal points.

+ 14.59   **Regroup** numbers as necessary.

16.66   Write the decimal point in the answer too.

Example 3

Subtract 12.04 – 3.98.

Regroup
Regroup again

1$\overset{1}{2}.\overset{9}{\cancel{0}}\overset{1}{4}$ You need to regroup from the ones place so you can subtract 8 in the hundredths place.

– 3.98

8.06

Estimating is important when you add or subtract decimals, as it will give you some idea of the size of a reasonable answer.

1   Rachel and Sam kept some tadpoles in a tank for their science project. They sketched the tadpoles and recorded the length of the body and tail (in cm) as they grew.

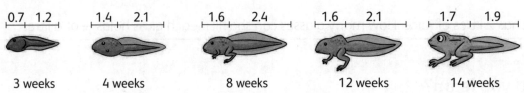

| 0.7 | 1.2 | 1.4 | 2.1 | 1.6 | 2.4 | 1.6 | 2.1 | 1.7 | 1.9 |

3 weeks   4 weeks   8 weeks   12 weeks   14 weeks

   a   Calculate the total length of the tadpoles at each state of growth.

   b   What is the difference in length between the 3-week stage and the 14-week stage?

2   Add.

   a 0.4 + 0.37   b 1 + 0.89   c 0.1 + 2.39   d 4.61 + 0.22
   e 0.3 + 13   f 21.3 + 34.24   g 2.48 + 2.78   h 5.24 + 6.67

3   Write in columns and add.

   a 18.22 + 71.66   b 0.47 + 13.3 + 8   c 17.54 + 11 + 0.7
   d 7 + 6.342 + 5.09   e 72.1 + 82.45 + 23.24 f 420.02 + 3.76 + 0.2

3   Subtract.

   a 65.47 − 13.25   b 14.26 − 8.01   c 59 − 36.05   d 1.75 − 0.6
   e 1.76 − 0.98   f 1.75 − 0.36   g 0.99 − 0.9   h 12.07 − 3.9

4   Round each decimal to the nearest whole number and estimate the answer before doing each
    of these calculations.

   a 3.63 + 9.8 + 6.21   b 14.3 + 6.7 + 9.69   c 98.76 − 54.12
   d 18.23 − 10.15   e 0.57 + 0.66 − 1 + 0.92 − 0.03   f 64.37 − 24.39 + 38.5

5   Mrs Joyner asked a group of students to add 0.43, 12.084 and 3.8.

Tamaya	Joshua	Kaylene	James	Linda
0.43	0.4300	043	0.43	0.430
12.084	12.084	12084	12.084	12.084
+ 3.8	2.7000	+ 38	3.8	3.800

   a Which student has set out the work correctly?
   b What have the others done incorrectly?

Problem-solving

6   Peter is 1.84 m tall. His sister is 1.6 m tall. How much taller is Peter?

7   A taxi travels 23.47 km on Monday, 38.05 km on Tuesday and 29 km on Wednesday. What is
    the total distance it travelled?

8   What is the perimeter of this shape?

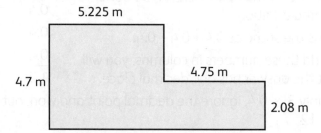

   5.225 m
   4.7 m
   4.75 m
   2.08 m

9   Mindy has a laptop and a printer next to each other on her desk. The desk is 1.2 m wide. The
    laptop is 32.5 cm wide and the printer is 0.48 m wide. Does she have enough space to put a
    0.5 m wide box next to them?

Multiplying decimals by 10, 100 or 1 000

You already know that when you multiply a whole number by 10, each **digit** moves one place to the left to make the answer ten times greater.

15 × 10 = 150

The same principle applies to decimals.

1.5 × 10 = 15   1.05 × 10 = 10.5

When you multiply or divide by 100 or 1 000, you move digits one place to the left for each power of ten. So for 100 you move two places and for 1 000 you move three places.

12 × 10 = 120   1.2 × 10 = 12
12 × 100 = 1 200   1.2 × 100 = 120
12 × 1 000 = 12 000   1.2 × 1 000 = 1 200

10 Multiply.

a 2.34 × 10	b 32.5 × 10	c 0.45 × 10	d 0.08 × 10
e 54.34 × 10	f 0.08 × 10	g 1.2 × 10	h 43.2 × 10
i 4.56 × 100	j 32.45 × 100	k 9.45 × 100	l 9.21 × 100
m 0.08 × 100	n 4.32 × 1 000	o 1.2 × 1 000	p 0.8 × 1 000
q 7.99 × 100	r 6.5 × 1 000	s 0.08 × 10	t 0.75 × 1 000

11 A builder requires 100 m of timber at $12.68 per metre. What will the timber cost?

12 The overall cost of a wedding reception for 100 guests was $12 345.50. What was the cost per guest?

13 Ten thousand people each paid $1.99 for a charity raffle ticket. How much money was raised through ticket sales?

Multiplying a decimal by a whole number

You can multiply decimals by whole numbers. To do this, you ignore the decimal point and multiply the **factors** as if they were whole numbers. Then you put back the decimal point in the product. Your answer will have the same number of **decimal places** as the decimal you multiplied. Look at this example to understand why.

Example 1

What is 3 × 0.4?

Remember that multiplication can be done as repeated addition.

3 × 0.4 is the same as 0.4 + 0.4 + 0.4.

If you add these numbers in columns, you will see that the answer has one decimal place.

$$\begin{array}{r} 0.4 \\ 0.4 \\ \underline{0.4} \\ 1.2 \end{array}$$

To multiply 3 × 0.4, ignore the decimal point and work out 3 × 4 = 12

The multiplication had a factor (0.4) with one decimal place, so the product will have one decimal place.

3 × 0.4 = 1.2

Example 2

If your decimal has two places, the product will also have two places.

Now consider 0.24 × 4.

If you add, you get:

The product must have two decimal places, so 24 × 4 = 96, and 0.24 × 4 = 0.96

$$\begin{array}{r} 0.24 \\ 0.24 \\ 0.24 \\ 0.24 \\ \hline 0.96 \end{array}$$

Example 3

Calculate 5 × 3.43.

5 × 3.43 There are two decimal places in the factors.

$$\begin{array}{r} {}^2 3^1 43 \\ \times \quad 5 \\ \hline 1\,715 \end{array}$$

Insert a decimal point so that the product has two decimal places:

So 5 × 3.43 = 17.15

14 Multiply.

a 2 × 0.6   b 6 × 0.9   c 3 × 3.2   d 5 × 4.1

e 2 × 0.3   f 5 × 0.1   g 7 × 0.4   h 8 × 1.12

i 0.7 × 8   j 0.09 × 3   k 7.89 × 4   l 70.41 × 3

15 Find the product of these numbers.

a 9 and 22.3   b 2.09 and 4   c 60.8 and 8   d 0.99 and 9

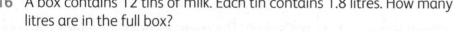

Problem-solving

16 A box contains 12 tins of milk. Each tin contains 1.8 litres. How many litres are in the full box?

17 A pen costs $4.55. How much would 8 pens cost?

18 Doctors have found that you can estimate the height to which a child will grow if you double the height they are when they are two years old.

a Estimate how tall each of these two-year olds will be in metres when they are fully grown.

b Which person do you think grew up to be a basketball champion? Why?

Dwight 88.9 cm

Usain 97.5 cm

Shelly-Anne 0.76 m

Al 104.14 m

What did you learn?

1 Micah bought three items costing $2.62, $1.89 and $2.00. How much change would he get if he paid with a $10.00 bill?

2 Asafa puts 450 g and 0.98 kg into a pan on a scale. The scale shows a mass of 1.45 kg. What is the mass of the pan?

3 Calculate.

a 0.25 × 100   b 1.2 × 10   c 23.09 × 10   d 0.08 × 100

4 Calculate.

a 3 × 0.65   b 9 × 3.45   c 8 × 23.98   d 9 × 15.99

C Calculate with percentages

Maths ideas

In this unit you will:
* calculate percentages of quantities
* learn about profit and loss and how to calculate these
* express profit or loss as a percentage
* solve problems involving percentages.

Explain

Per cent means 'out of a hundred'. So, 3% means 3 out of every hundred. Mathematically, this is $\frac{3}{100}$ of a quantity. For example:

3% of 200 = $\frac{3}{100}$ of 200, and 3% of 350 = $\frac{3}{100}$ of 350.

You already know that the word 'of' tells you to multiply:

$\frac{3}{100}$ of 200 = $\frac{3}{100} \times \frac{200}{1} = \frac{600}{100} \div \frac{100}{100} = 6$

So, 3% of 200 = 6

$\frac{3}{100}$ of 350 = $\frac{3}{100} \times \frac{350}{1} = \frac{1\,050}{100} \div \frac{10}{10}$

$= \frac{105}{10} = 10\frac{5}{10} = 10\frac{1}{2}$

So, 3% of 350 = $10\frac{1}{2}$

Key words

per cent	selling price
reduce	profit
increase	loss
cost price	percentage

1   Calculate.
   a   2% of 200   b   20% of 600   c   50% of 40   d   10% of 80
   e   75% of 50   f   5% of 60   g   100% of 40   h   15% of 90

2   A shoe store has some pairs of shoes that are not selling. The owner decides to **reduce** the price by 20% to try and sell them. Work out the reduced price of each pair of shoes.

a

Was $120
Less 20%
Now

b

Was $280
Less 20%
Now

c

Was $195
Less 20%
Now

d

Was $220
Less 20%
Now

3   A shop decides to **increase** the price of furniture by 15%. Work out the new price of these items:
   a   a table that was $600   b   a chair that was $260.

Problem-solving

4   Mrs Sinclair has a 280 m² plot. She uses 40% of it to grow bananas, 30% to grow vegetables, 20% for a chicken coop and 10% for flowers. Work out the area of land used for each purpose in square metres.

5   20 000 workers were employed in the bauxite industry. The price of bauxite dropped and 15% of the workers were retrenched. How many people were retrenched?

6   Zayn had a plank that was 3 m long. He cut off 32% off the length. How many centimetres did he cut off?

7   Customs duty on imported cars is 28%. What duty would you pay on a car imported from the United States that costs $12 000?

Profit and loss

Explain

Jean bought a CD player that cost $60 on sale. Her **cost price** was $60.

She sold the CD player for $80. This is her **selling price**.

Jean sold the CD player for $20 more than it cost her. This means she made a profit of $20. **Profit** is the amount of money you make over and above the cost price.

Profit = selling price − cost price

Sometimes things are sold for less than they cost.

Tony bought shoes that cost $120, but they were slightly too small and hurt his feet. He sold them to a friend for $100.

Tony's cost price was $120 and his selling price was $100. He sold them for $20 less than he paid. This is called a **loss**.

Loss = cost price − selling price

8   Work out the missing values in this table.

Cost price	Selling price	Profit
$100	$120	a
$75	$100	b
$75	c	$15
$120	d	$30
e	$80	$10
f	$150	$50

9   Calculate the loss for each sale and the total loss.

Bought for	Sold for	Loss
$100	$80	
$500	$420	
$196.50	$150	
$1 250	$750	
Total loss		

Profit and loss as a percentage

Explain

Once you have worked out the amount of profit or loss (in dollars or cents), you can calculate the **percentage** profit or loss.

Percentage profit = $\dfrac{\text{profit}}{\text{cost price}} \times \dfrac{100}{1}$

Percentage loss = $\dfrac{\text{loss}}{\text{cost price}} \times \dfrac{100}{1}$

Example 1

Sheila bought a calculator for $60 and sold it for $75. What was her percentage profit?

Profit = $75 − $60 = $15

Percentage profit = $\dfrac{15}{60} \times \dfrac{100}{1} = \dfrac{1\,500}{60} \div \dfrac{60}{60} = 25\%$

127

Example 2

Marcus bought a bike for $250 and sold it 6 weeks later for $200. Express his loss as a percentage.

Loss = $250 − $200 = $50

Percentage loss = $\frac{50}{250} \times \frac{100}{1} = \frac{5\,000}{250} = \frac{250}{250} = 20\%$

10 For each item in the table, calculate the profit or loss and express it as a percentage.

Item	a	b	c	d	e	f	g
Cost price	$20	$50	$90	$80	$200	$1 200	$480
Selling price	$25	$30	$108	$72	$188	$1 450	$360

Problem-solving

11 Al bought a pair of shoes for $85 and sold them for $120.
   a What profit did he make in dollars?   b What was his percentage profit?

12 A stall owner bought mangoes for 50 cents each. They were over-ripe, so the stall owner sold them for $0.30 each. Calculate the loss on 25 mangoes and express it as a percentage.

13 Nick sold a book to his friend for $5.00 and lost $4.00 on the sale.
   a What was the cost price of the book?   b Express Nick's loss as a percentage.

14 Mrs James bought a packet of 24 cards for $30. She sold each card for $2.25.
   a What was Mrs James' total profit?   b Express this as a percentage.

Challenge

15 Mr Blaize tries to make 25% profit on everything he sells in his store. Work out what he would need to charge for each of these items to make that profit?
   a Bicycles that cost $175   b Inner tubes that cost $12   c Tyres that cost $45

What did you learn?

1 Calculate.
   a 5% of 450   b 12% of 80   c 29% of 300   d 120% of 100

2 Write your own definitions of each term.
   a Profit   b Loss   c Cost price   d Selling price

3 Calculate the profit or loss in each case as a percentage.
   a I bought materials for a total of $25 and paid an employee $45 to make a table. I sold the table for $95.
   b I sold a car for $1 480. The car originally cost me $2 999.

Topic 13 Review

Key ideas and concepts

Give examples using numbers to show that you understand each of these concepts and to summarise what you learnt in this topic.

1 Adding and subtracting fractions with different denominators

2 Calculating a fraction of a quantity

3 Multiplying fractions

4 Dividing a fraction by a whole number

5 Adding and subtracting decimals

6 Multiplying a decimal by a whole number

7 Finding a percentage of a quantity

8 Calculating profit or loss in dollars

9 Calculating percentage profit or loss

Think, talk, write ...

Discuss these questions in your groups.

1 Why is it important for a business to make a profit?

2 Why do businesses sometimes make a loss on some items?

3 How does a business know whether it is making a profit or loss?

4 A vendor asks if it is better to sell a few T-shirts and make a big profit on each sale or to sell lots of T-shirts and make a smaller profit on each sale. What would you advise? Why?

Quick check

1 What fraction is:

   a $\frac{1}{4}$ more than $\frac{1}{3}$?

   b $\frac{1}{2}$ less than $\frac{5}{8}$?

   c $1\frac{1}{2}$ greater than $2\frac{1}{6}$?

   d $2\frac{1}{4}$ smaller than $3\frac{1}{9}$?

   e 3 times $\frac{3}{7}$?

   f $\frac{1}{4}$ of $\frac{3}{9}$?

2 Calculate.

   a $23.47 + 38.43 + 13$

   b $12.09 + 14.765$

   c $143.09 - 14.245$

   d $35 - 19.99$

   e 4×12.4

   f 9×34.09

3 Write as a percentage.

   a 14 out of 15

   b 25 out of 50

   c $\frac{17}{20}$

4 Calculate.

   a 12% of 350

   b 9% of 500

   c 2% of 12 000

5 1.05 litres of water are poured from a container that holds 2 litres. How much water is left?

6 Mrs Baker buys mangoes for $6.00 per dozen. She sells them for $1.25 each. One afternoon she sells 54 mangoes. Calculate her total profit and express it as a percentage of the cost price.

7 Make up three multi-step problems involving money amounts. Swap problems with a partner and solve each other's problems.

Teaching notes

Time

* Students already know how to tell and write time (on analogue and digital clocks) using the 12-hour system. This year they will learn about the universal 24-hour system of telling time, which allows times to be written without a.m. or p.m. notifications.

* Students are probably already familiar with 24-hour time, as they would have seen these on mobile phones, computer screens and airport notice boards.

* The duration of an event is how long it takes. An event that starts at 5 and ends at 5.30 has a duration of 30 minutes. Counting on by adding first the hours and then the minutes is a useful way of working out duration.

* Time is not metric, so students need to remember the relationships between units when they calculate with time. Half an hour can be written as 0.5 hours, but this means 30 minutes and not 50 minutes.

Money

* Money calculations can be treated like any other decimal calculation, as long as students understand that money amounts always have two decimal places, so we write $2.50 and not $2.5.

* The concepts of cost price, selling price, profit, loss and discount were taught in Topic 13, when students worked with percentages. You may need to revise these if students don't fully understand them.

* Money is a mathematical concept that has direct relevance to the students' everyday lives. It is important that you acknowledge this in the classroom. For example, in some countries, small denomination coins are being removed from circulation. Similarly, it is becoming less and less common for people to use cheques or to go into the bank to deposit or withdraw money. Most people will use a bank card and an automatic bank machine.

Temperature

* Students should be familiar with the concept of temperature and how it is measured.

* The focus this year is on the Celsius scale. Students need to work with real thermometers to estimate and read temperatures.

* Some thermometers, like clocks, can be digital. Try to show students both the analogue and digital versions.

A

Time	Flight	To / Via	Gate	Status
10:15	EK 342	Kuala Lumpur	B14	Boarding
10:15	QF 8412	Sydney	B15	
10:15	MK 913	Mauritius	B32	Boarding
10:20	EK 334	Manila	B10	Gate Open
10:20	EK 851	Doha	C20	Boarding
10:25	QF 8434	Brisbane	A12	
10:30	EK 586	Dhaka	B25	Gate Open
10:30	QF 8723	Addis Ababa	B16	
10:30	EK 725	Dar Es Salaam	B22	
10:30	EK 783	Lagos	A7	
10:35	QF 8719	Nairobi	B24	
10:40	SA 7165	Durban	C7	
10:45	QF 8424	Perth	C18	
10:50	EK 362	Guangzhou	B19	
10:50	EK 778	Cape Town	B4	
11:00	EK 358	Jakarta	B27	
11:10	EK 308	Beijing	A5	
11:45	EK 370	Bangkok	A3	
12:00	EK 871	Kuwait	A1	
12:10	EK 031	London Heathrow	A21	
12:20	MK 9936	Colombo	A16	
12:45	EK 378	Phuket	A23	
13:10	EK 502	Mumbai	B18	

This is a display board seen at a large international airport. What information does it give? How are times shown on the board? Why do you think they are shown in this way?

B

Mrs Paulwell received this bill at a restaurant. How much did the food and drinks cost? What is a service charge? How is it worked out on this bill? Mrs Paulwell paid the bill using her bank card. How does the restaurant get the money?

Think, talk and write

A **Time** *(pages 132–134)*

1 How long do these activities usually take? Write your answer in hours or minutes.
   a Watching TV
   b Drinking a glass of water
   c Putting on your clothes in the morning
   d Playing on a computer, phone or tablet
   e Playing a ball game such as cricket or netball

2 What unit of time describes:
   a 10 decades?
   b 12 months?
   c 24 hours?

B **Money** *(pages 135–137)*

1 Select one coin and one banknote used in your country. Describe each one and list the information that you can find on it.

2 Work in pairs.

$2 048.55	$98 499.99
$15 386.50	$9 500.00

   a Say each amount.
   b Write the amounts in order from least to most money.
   c If these are prices, what do you think are the items that cost each amount?

C **Temperature** *(page 138)*

1 Match each item to an approximate temperature from the box. Write your answers in a table.

100 °C	60 °C	25 °C	37 °C	0 °C

   a Healthy body temperature
   b Boiling point of water
   c Freezing point of water
   d The temperature in the Eastern Caribbean in winter
   e Temperature of a cup of warm tea.

C

15:31   27°C

Average fuel economy

15.7

km/L

Ⓐ 52.1 km
    3291 km

Look at this display from a car dashboard. What measurements are given? Which measurement tells you what the temperature is outside the vehicle? How do you know this is a temperature reading? Is this a cool or a warm temperature?

A Time

This is an **analogue clock**. It shows the time using an hour hand and a minute hand.

This clock shows 25 past 2. You can't tell from the clock alone whether this is 25 past 2 in the afternoon or 25 past 2 in the morning.

A **digital clock** shows time using only numbers.

Hour

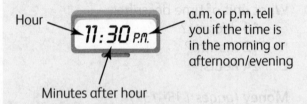

a.m. or p.m. tell you if the time is in the morning or afternoon/evening

Minutes after hour

11:30 p.m. means half past 11 in the evening.
11:30 a.m. means half past 11 in the morning.

This clock uses the **24-hour time** system. Instead of switching from a.m. to p.m. after 12 o'clock, the hours continue to 13:00 (1 o'clock), 14:00 (2 o'clock), and so on, up to 24:00 (12 midnight). On the 24-hour clock, each day starts at 00:00, which is the same time as 24:00 or midnight. The clock in the picture shows 23:30, which is the same as 11:30 p.m.

Maths ideas

In this unit you will:
* revise what you already know about time
* use the 24-hour system to tell and write times
* create and solve problems involving time.

Key words

analogue clock
digital clock
24-hour time
duration
elapsed

1   Write the time shown on each clock.

a    b    c    d

2   Write these times as they would appear on a digital clock.
   a   23 minutes past 5 in the afternoon
   b   Half past one in the morning
   c   Five minutes before six o'clock in the morning

3   Write these times using the 24-hour system.
   a   12:45 p.m.   b   2:55 a.m.   c   01:15 p.m.   d   9:28 p.m.

4   Write these times using the 12-hour system. Include a.m. or p.m.
   a   08:18   b   16:00   c   06:20   d   13:30
   e   01:30   f   18:15   g   19:48   h   00:30

5   Arrange these times from earliest to latest.

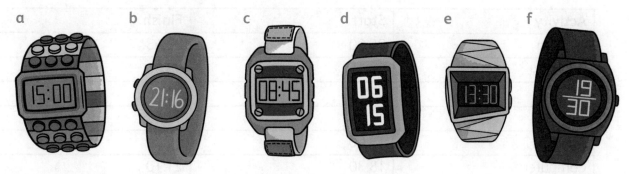

a	b	c	d	e	f

Explain

Think about this question: 'How long does it take?' The answer to this question tells you the **duration** of an event. The duration tells you how long something takes from start to finish.

Example 1

A TV programme started at 4:15 p.m. and ended at 4:50 p.m. How long was the programme?

You can count on from the starting time to the finishing time to work out the duration:

```
      +15    +20
   4:15   4:30   4:50
```

15 + 20 = 35 minutes

In this example, you could also choose to subtract the starting time from the finishing time to work out the duration. Treat the hours and minutes as separate units.

4 h	50 min
4 h	15 min
0 h	35 min

Example 2

Elapsed time is the time that passes from the beginning of an event until it finishes.

Mila starts her piano lesson at 3:30 p.m. The lesson lasts 45 minutes. What time does it finish?

	Hours	Minutes	
	3	30	
+		45	
=	3	75	60 minutes = 1 hour
			75 – 60 = 15
=	4 hours 15 minutes		

She finishes at 4:15 p.m.

The start time is 3:30 p.m. The elapsed time is 45 minutes. The end time is 4:15 p.m.

133

1 The table shows how long Nathan spent on different activities.

Activity	Start	Finish
Jogging	06:00	06:45
Breakfast	08:15	08:30
Library	09: 35	11:30
Lunch	12:10	13:00
Football	15:00	16:20
Computer	18:30	21:10

a How long did he spend jogging?

b After leaving the library, how long did he have to wait before football started?

c What did he do between the time he left the library and the time football started? How long did this take?

d Which activity took the longest time? How long did it take?

e Which activity took the least time? How long did it take?

2 Mrs Christians received 5 items in the post on 24 February. These are the postmarks on the items (a postmark shows you when something was posted).

a Write down where each item was posted and when it was posted.

b How long did each item take to reach Mrs Christians?

3 Work out when each activity finished.

a I go for a run at 11:25 a.m. I run for an hour and ten minutes.

b A TV show starts at 8:05 p.m. It lasts for 45 minutes.

c Sports day starts at 8:15 a.m. It finishes $5\frac{1}{2}$ hours later.

4 Work out the starting time of each activity.

a I get home at 5:10 p.m. after a 55-minute car journey. What time did I start the journey?

b A movie finishes at 7:55 p.m. It was 2 hours 35 minutes long. What time did it start?

5 Work out how long each activity took.

a James put a cake in the oven at 11:07 a.m. and took it out at 11:42 a.m. How long did he bake it for?

b Rebecca started a car journey at 10:32 a.m. and arrived at her destination at 12:05 p.m. How long did the journey take?

c Jenna started her run at 6:20 p.m. and finished at 7:07 p.m. How long did she run for?

What did you learn?

A flight left Canada at 10:05 and arrived in Antigua at 16:30.

1 Write the departure and arrival times using a.m. and p.m.

2 How long did the flight take?

3 The flight landed 45 minutes late. What time should it have arrived?

B Money

Explain

We use money in our daily lives to pay for things. It is important to know how much to pay during **transactions** and what notes and coins you can use to make up different amounts. You also need to know how to work out **change** when you give someone more money than the total **cost** of the bill.

You can calculate with money in the same way that you work with decimals. Remember, though, that written amounts in dollars and cents have two decimal places: we write $5.20, not $5.2.

Maths ideas

In this unit you will:
* read and write amounts of money
* calculate costs and change
* understand more about how money is used in daily life.

Key words

transactions

change

cost

1   Look at the notes and coins.

  a   From which country is each piece of currency?
  b   Are all the dollars shown worth the same amount? Explain.

2   Write these amounts using numbers and symbols.
  a   Four thousand three hundred and eighty-six dollars and sixty-five cents
  b   Twenty-six thousand seven hundred and fifty dollars and eighty cents

3   The answers to some money calculations are shown on these screens.

| 5.9 | 0.65 | 125.5 | 50.05 | 89 |

  a   Write each money amount in words.
  b   What would you enter into a calculator to work out $15.75 plus 89 cents?
  c   Three friends share the cost of a meal equally. When they divide the bill by three they get an amount of 15.7266666667. How much should each person pay? Why?

4   How would you make up these amounts using the fewest possible number of coins and notes?
   a $10.35   b $99.55   c $107.90
   d $509.80   e $750.00   f $1 200.00

5   Use any combination of $100, $50 and $20 bills to work out what notes each person has in their wallet.
   a   Bonnie has 5 notes that total exactly $240.
   b   Simon has 6 notes. The total is more than $150 but less than $300.

6   Pedro sells second-hand goods at a market. The picture shows what he has for sale and gives the price of each item.

Calculate the total cost of the following combinations of items.

   a   A + D   b   E + F   c   B + C + D
   d   C + E + F   e   A + B + C   f   C + F + G

   g   If you bought items D and F and gave Pedro a $50 bill, how much change would you get?

   h   A customer wanted to buy all the items on display. Pedro offered her a 10% discount on the total price.
      i   What is the total price of all the items?
      ii   Calculate 10% of the total amount.
   i   What would the customer have to pay after the discount?

Think and talk

When Pedro has only one or two items left he sometimes sells them at cost price or at a loss. Why do you think he does this?

7   Sandra is awarded a scholarship to study in New York. She is given a room in a dorm and US$200 to decorate it. She gets the following quote from student affairs:

2 tins of paint	@ $6.75 each
4 rolls of wallpaper	@ $3.64 per roll
10 square metres of carpet	@ $8.23 per square metre
6 metres of curtaining	@ $6.86 per metre
3 hours of labour	@ $8.50 per hour

a   How much does the quote come to in total?

b   How much will Sandra have left if she pays this amount?

c   Sandra wants to buy bed linen for $17.50 and a shelf for $5.00. Can she afford this? If so, how much will she have left over?

8   Danny bought a bicycle for $150. Two months later he sold it for $85. How much was his loss?

9   The Music Store sells CDs for EC$60 each. On Saturdays the store offers a discount of 10%. June bought 5 CDs on Saturday morning. How much did she pay?

10   Mrs Baker sells mangoes in the market. She buys the mangoes from a farmer at $6.00 per dozen. She sells them at $1.00 each. If she sells 54 mangoes, how much profit does she make?

11   The cost price of a television is $850.00. The store sells it and makes a profit of $78. What is the selling price?

12   A woman works for a wage of $45 per day, Monday to Friday. If she works at weekends, she is paid $10 per hour.

a   How much would the woman earn if she worked Monday, Wednesday and Friday only in one week?

b   The next week she works Monday, Tuesday, Wednesday, Thursday, Friday and for 4 hours on Saturday. How much does she earn?

13   Which of the following is the most economical buy?
Show how you work this out.

a   6 sausages for $11.99, or 4 sausages for $10.00?

b   250 grams rice for $6.98, or 500 grams for $13.59?

c   5 litres fruit punch for $6.99, or 15 litres for $21.99?

What did you learn?

1   Write each of these amounts in dollars using symbols and numbers.

a   Twelve dollars fifty

b   Seventy-nine cents

c   7 cents

2   What is:

a $3.65 – $1.25?

b $45 – $1.50?

c $5 – 45¢?

C Temperature

Temperature is measured using a thermometer. The **Celsius scale** gives the temperature in **degrees** Celsius (°C). Water freezes at 0 °C and it boils at 100 °C. Your normal body temperature is between 36 °C and 37 °C.

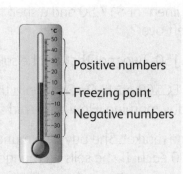

Positive numbers

Freezing point

Negative numbers

When it is very cold (for example, in a freezer or in Antarctica), temperatures can drop below 0 °C. A temperature of −1 °C is one degree less than zero, or 1 degree below zero. A temperature of −10 °C is ten degrees below zero. Remember that when you work with negative numbers, the greater the number after the minus sign, the colder the temperature.

Maths ideas

In this unit you will:
* revisit temperature in degrees Celsius.

Key words

Celsius scale

degrees

digital

Example

Katy makes ice-cream. The temperature of her mixture is 19 °C. She puts it in the freezer overnight. The next day, the ice-cream is frozen and she measures its temperature as −5 °C. What was the change in temperature?

$$5 \qquad 19 \qquad 5 + 19 = 24$$

−5   0   19   There was a change in temperature of 24 °C.

1   Write the temperature shown on each thermometer in degrees Celsius.

a

b

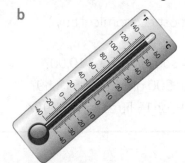

c

2   What will the temperature be on each thermometer if it drops 12 degrees?

Problem-solving

3   John makes ice. The water is 23 °C when he pours it into the trays for freezing. The next day, the ice is at −10 °C. What was the temperature change?

What did you learn?

1   If the temperature is 20 °C and it increases to 32 °C, how many degrees has it increased by?

2   If the temperature is 12 °C and it goes down 23 °C, what is the new temperature?

Topic 14 Review

Key ideas and concepts

Copy and complete these sentences to summarise what you learnt in this topic.

1 Three important ideas/things I learnt about time are _____, _____ _____, but the most important thing I learnt is _____.

2 Three important ideas/things about money are _____, _____ _____, but the most important thing I learnt is _____.

3 When you work with temperature, you need to know _____ and you must remember that _____.

Think, talk, write ...

What do these expressions about time mean? Write your own explanations. You can use a dictionary or the internet to help you.

There is no time like the present.	I am just killing time.	We should call it a day.	It is crunch time.	This can help you save time.

Do you know some everyday expressions that people use to talk about money or describe temperature? Write these as speech bubbles in your maths journal.

Quick check

1 Write down the matching pairs of times.

> 8 o'clock at night   ten to 1   9:00 p.m.   18:00   6:00 p.m.
> half past 12   20:00   00:30   12:50   21:00

2 My grandfather has lived for 5 decades and 9 years. How old is he?

3 Ali started her homework at 3:25 p.m. and finished at 4:50 p.m. How long did she spend on it?

4 Make up five word problems involving money amounts. Write the solutions on a separate sheet. Exchange problems with another student and try to solve each other's questions. Check each other's answers and discuss any that are incorrect.

5 Give any two typical temperatures in °C (for example, body temperature, or the freezing or boiling point of water).

6 A scientist made a solution that measures 25.5 °C. Then she lowered the temperature to −12 °C. What was the temperature change?

Problem-solving

7 On a winter's day in the Netherlands, the temperature is 7 °C during the day. It drops to −12 °C at night. What is the change?

8 In Lhasa, Tibet, the temperature can be 29 °C in summer, and can fall as low as −16 °C in winter. Calculate the change between the summer high and the winter low.

Topic

15 Data handling (2)

Teaching notes

Organising and representing data

* Students have already worked with tallies and frequency tables and know how to organise data in categories and in groups.

* Once you have organised a data set, you can represent it graphically. Different types of graph are useful for different kinds of data. Pictographs and bar graphs are useful for comparing data in categories. Line graphs are useful for data that shows a change over time.

* The scale of the graph is important. Students need to use an appropriate scale for the data set they have.

Line graphs

* Line graphs are used to show changes over time. For example, a line graph can show how a baby's mass increases from birth to one year, or how the value of a new car decreases over time.

* A line graph needs labelled axes. Time is normally shown on the horizontal axis.

* Points are plotted on the graph and joined with a line to show changes in the data. A line that slopes upwards shows an increase and a line that slopes downwards shows a decrease.

Interpreting graphs

* The heading, labels and scale (interval) used in a graph are important. Students need to read these carefully to make sense of the data set.

Probability

* The theoretical probability of something happening, for example, a coin landing on heads or tails, can be worked out mathematically. There is an equal chance of a coin landing on heads or tails.

* In reality, however, you might get tails ten times in a row and no heads. This is called experimental probability. If you toss the coin thousands of times, the experimental outcomes will get closer and closer to the mathematical probability.

A

Mr Richardson records how much rain falls at his home using a rain gauge. What is the best way for him to collect and record the data? What type of graph could he use to show the data for a year? Why?

B

Sam is trying to decide which type of graph to draw to show a set of data. He knows about pictographs, bar graphs and line graphs. What should he consider when he is making a decision about what graph to draw? Suggest data that is suitable for each type of graph.

C

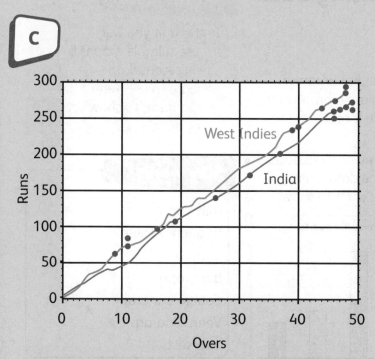

Have you seen graphs like this one while watching sport? How do you know what the graph shows? Which team has won this match?

A **Organising and representing data** (pages 142–144)

1 Name three ways of collecting data.
2 What does it mean to organise data?
3 What kinds of graphs have you learnt about and drawn?
4 How are a bar graph and a pictograph similar? How do they differ?

B **Drawing graphs** (pages 145–146)

1 Draw a flow diagram to show the steps you would follow to draw a bar graph.
2 Why is it important to label a graph clearly?

C **Interpreting bar and line graphs** (pages 147–148)

1 Work in pairs. Discuss what these terms mean and how they help you make sense of a graph.
  a Heading
  b Scale
  c Labels
  d Interval
2 How do bar graphs show data? What does it mean if one bar is longer than another?

D

Imagine that you roll a green dice and a red dice. In how many ways can you get a total of two? In how many ways can you get a total of seven? Do you think the chance of getting a double six is less than the chance of getting a six with any other number? Why or why not?

D **Probability** (pages 149–150)

Think about the weather conditions for your country for tomorrow.

1 What weather conditions are possible?
2 What weather conditions do you expect? Why?
3 Are there any weather conditions that are impossible for your country for tomorrow? Explain your thinking.

A Organising and representing data

Explain

Tally charts and frequency tables can be used to organise data. Once data has been organised, you can use a graph or other diagram to represent the data and make it easier to see important information.

Before you draw a graph (or other diagram) you need to decide which type of graph is most appropriate for the data. Think about the purpose of the graph and what you want to show.

Bar graphs are useful when you want to compare data in different categories.

A teacher did a survey in class about students' favourite sport.

The bar graph shows the results. Which sport is the most popular?

The teacher decides that the bar graph does not give an accurate enough picture of his

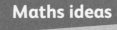

Favourite sports

students' interest in sports, as the data for the boys and the girls differs a lot. So he decides to use a double bar graph to show the data. Note that the graph has a key that shows which data is for girls and which is for boys.

The graph clearly shows that softball is the girls' favourite sport. They boys' favourite sport is basketball.

A double bar graph displays information about two related sets of data. It shows the data for two different groups, for example, girls and boys, but with the same categories. This allows you to compare the data for the different groups.

The bars can be vertical or horizontal.

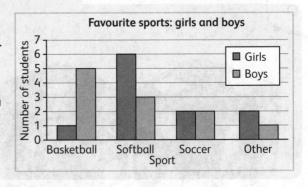

Favourite sports: girls and boys

1   Lucy is having a party. She did a survey among her friends and family to find out what kind of music they like. The results are shown in this double bar graph.

   a   What is the favourite and the least favourite music among the children?

   b   What is the favourite and the least favourite music among the adults?

   c   What is the best music to choose so that both adults and children have a good time?

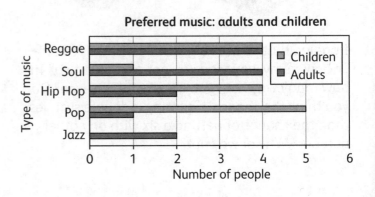

Preferred music: adults and children

2 A mathematics teacher surprised his class with an unprepared test. He then told the class they would write another test in a week's time. The results of the two tests are shown below for one group of students.

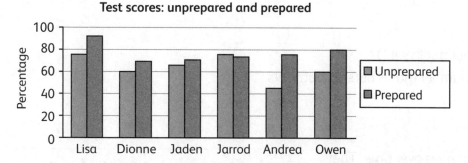

Test scores: unprepared and prepared

Write down ten observations you can make from the graph.

Explain

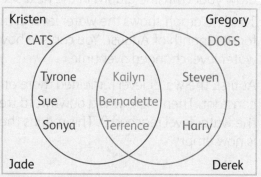

James did a survey to find out whether students had a pet dog or cat. He found that some students had a dog, some had a cat, some had both and some had neither.

He decided to use a **Venn diagram** to represent this data.

The Venn diagram shows that three students, Tyrone, Sue and Sonya, have only a cat. Steven and Harry have only a dog.

Kailyn, Bernadette and Terrence have both a cat and a dog. Since these three students are included in both sets, their names are placed where the two circles overlap or **intersect**.

The names of students who do not own any cats or dogs are placed outside both circles, in this case Kristen, Jade, Gregory and Derek.

In this Venn diagram, there are two overlapping sets:

CATS = {Bernadette, Kailyn, Sonya, Sue, Terrence, Tyrone} and

DOGS = {Bernadette, Harry, Kailyn, Steven, Terrence}

In mathematical notation, we can say:

* Sue $\in$ CATS means that 'Sue' is an element, or member, of the set CATS.
* CATS $\cup$ DOGS is the union of both sets and includes every element in both sets.
* CATS $\cup$ DOGS = {Bernadette, Harry, Kailyn, Sonya, Steven, Sue, Terrence, Tyrone}
* CATS $\cap$ DOGS is the intersection of both sets which includes only the elements that overlap.
* CATS $\cap$ DOGS = {Bernadette, Kailyn, Terrence}

3 This Venn diagram shows the courses that students are taking in art class.

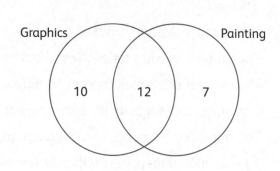

   a How many students are taking graphics and painting?

   b How many students are taking graphics only?

   c How many students are taking painting?

   d How many students are there in art class altogether?

143

4   Here are two sets of numbers, C = {1, 3, 5, 7, 9} and D = {2, 3, 5, 7}.

   a   True or false: 3 ∈ C?

   b   True or false: 1 ∈ D?

   c   What is C ∪ D?

   d   What is C ∩ D?

   e   What is in set C but not in set D?

   f   Write down one number that is outside both sets.

Explain

Line graphs can show changes over time. They allow you to see overall trends such as an increase or decrease in data over time. (You will learn to draw your own line graphs in the next section.)

This line graph shows the water level in a reservoir for the month of August. You can see how the water level changed over time.

At first, the water level remained more or less constant. Then there was a downward trend until the water level reached 0. This means the reservoir is now empty.

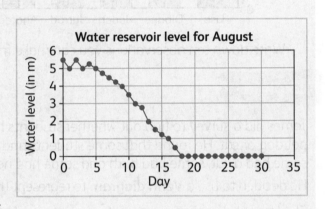

5   This line graph shows Mrs Smith's electricity charges for the first six months of the year. Study the graph. Then say whether each statement is true or false.

   a   Electricity charges went up after April.

   b   Charges were stable between March and April.

   c   Charges were at their lowest after March.

   d   The electricity charges varied by $100.00 only.

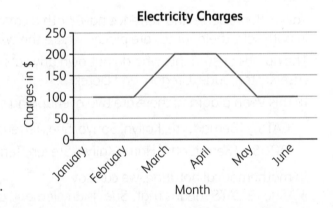

What did you learn?

Which type of graph or diagram would you use to best illustrate the following? Give a reason for each choice.

1   The number of books checked out at the school library per month for the past year

2   The number of votes for each candidate running for president

3   The number of internet users in 10 different countries

4   The amount of sugar in different types of food

5   The number of students who use a laptop, tablet or both

6   The number of teenagers with cell phones in your country over the past 10 years

B Drawing graphs

Maths ideas

In this unit you will:
* draw bar and line graphs to represent data sets.

Explain

You already know how to draw pictographs and bar graphs. Read through this information to remind you of the important features of a bar graph.

Jessica did a survey to find out where students did their homework. She used a frequency table to organise the data and drew a bar graph to represent it.

Key words

line graph   scale
horizontal axis   interval
vertical axis   plot

Room	Number of students
Study	5
Bedroom	9
Lounge	21
Kitchen	16
Other	4

A **line graph** also has a heading and two labelled axes. The **horizontal axis** is used for the time and the **vertical axis** has a **scale** to show the quantity that changes.

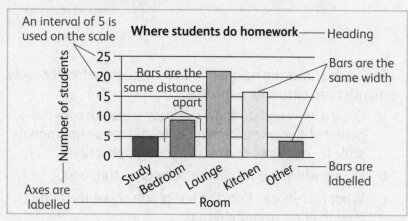

An interval of 5 is used on the scale. Where students do homework — Heading. Bars are the same distance apart. Bars are the same width. Axes are labelled. Bars are labelled. Number of students. Room.

Read through this information to learn how to draw a line graph.

Troy recorded how far he ran in a minute. He wanted to draw a line graph to show the data.

Step 1: Look at the two sets of numbers to decide on a suitable scale for the axes. Remember the vertical axis must start at 0. The time is shown on the horizontal axis.

Time passed (in seconds)	Distance covered (in metres)
10	40
20	75
30	105
40	125
50	150
60	165

The total distance is 165 metres, so the vertical scale needs to go to at least 165 metres. An **interval** of 20 metres would work well. A smaller interval would mean too many labels on the axis.

In this data set, it makes sense to have an interval of 10 seconds on the horizontal scale, as this scale is used in the table.

Step 2: Label the axes and mark the intervals on each scale. Include the units if you are working with measurements.

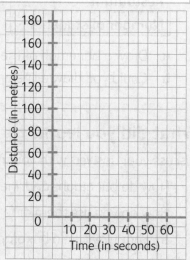

Step 3: **Plot** the points. Move up from the time and across from the distance and make a dot where the two measurements meet on the grid (think of these as coordinates).

Step 4: **Join** the points. Use a ruler to draw straight lines that join the points in order.

Step 5: **Give** the graph a suitable title.

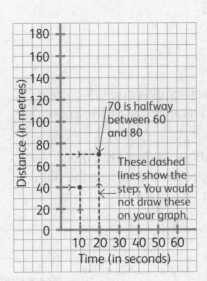

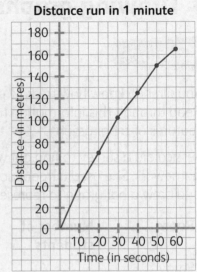

Distance run in 1 minute

1 The table shows the height of a baby in centimetres for every month from birth until 6 months.

a Draw a line graph to show the baby's growth over the period of 6 months. Remember to choose an appropriate scale for each axis and to give your graph a title.

b During which month did the baby grow the most?

c What can you tell from the line graph about the baby's growth during months 4 to 6?

Birth	Height
1 month	53 cm
2 months	57 cm
3 months	60 cm
4 months	62 cm
5 months	64 cm
6 months	66 cm

2 The table shows the amount of rain (in millimetres) that fell in Dolphin Bay during 5 days.

a Draw a suitable graph to show the data.

b Why did you choose this type of graph?

Monday	12
Tuesday	8.5
Wednesday	13.5
Thursday	9
Friday	8.5

3 The information in this table shows the types of restaurant students in a class prefer.

Restaurant	Pizza	Chinese	Mexican	Seafood	Burgers
Number of students					

a Draw a bar graph of the data in your exercise book.

b Could you draw a line graph to show this data? Give a reason for your answer.

What did you learn?

Discuss your answers with your partner.

1 How do bar graphs and line graphs look different?

2 How do you use them differently?

3 In what ways are a bar graph and a line graph the same?

C Interpreting bar and line graphs

Explain

To **interpret** a graph and understand what it shows we have to read it carefully.

* Read the **heading** to find out what the graph shows.
* Read the **labels** on the axes to see what data is shown and what scale is used.
* Look for **patterns** or **trends** in the data.
* Think about what might be causing the patterns or trends and draw **conclusions** based on what you can see.

Maths ideas

In this unit you will:
* read and interpret data shown on different types of graphs.

Key words

interpret	patterns
heading	trends
labels	conclusions

Example

What does this pictograph show?

Playground litter before, during and after an anti-litter campaign at school

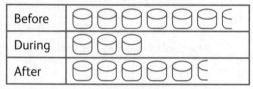

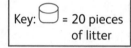

Key: ⌷ = 20 pieces of litter

The graph shows that there were 130 pieces of litter before the campaign. During the campaign, the amount of litter went down to 60 pieces, suggesting that the campaign was quite successful. However, afterwards, the number of pieces of litter increased again, but not to the same high level as before. This suggests some people learnt from the campaign and stopped littering, but many forgot once it was over. It might be useful to have an anti-litter campaign regularly to see if that makes a bigger difference over time.

1 Study the graph.

   a What does the title tell you about the graph?

   b What is shown on each axis?

   c What does it mean when the line on a line graph goes down?

   d This park introduced specialist anti-poaching patrols during this period. When do you think they did this? Why?

   e Describe the trend shown on the graph.

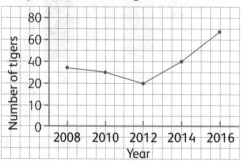

Tiger numbers in Rangata Forest Park

2 This graph shows how long students spent washing their hands after they used the toilets at school.

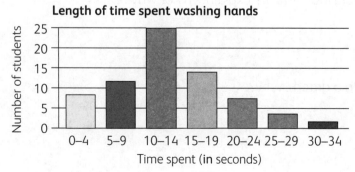

Length of time spent washing hands

    a How much time did most students spend washing their hands?

    b How many students spent less than 4 seconds washing their hands?

    c The World Health Organisation guidelines say you should wash your hands with soap and water for at least 20 seconds to prevent the spread of diseases. How well does this group of students meet those guidelines?

    d Does the graph give you information about students who didn't wash their hands at all?

    e How would you find out whether students at your school meet the health guidelines?

3 Mrs James wants to buy a new mobile phone and she sees this graph in an advert.

    a What does this graph show?

    b What happens to the cost if you talk for more than 250 minutes per month?

    c Mrs James doesn't make many calls. She estimates that she probably talks for about 50 minutes per month. Do you think this is a good option for her? What other information should she gather before deciding?

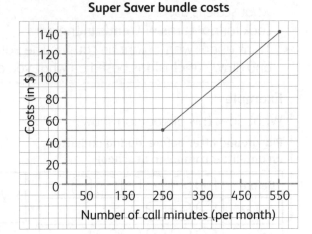

Super Saver bundle costs

4 Study the graph shown here and write notes describing what it shows.

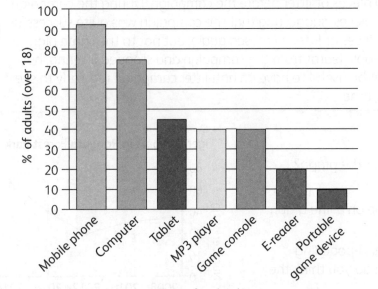

Most commonly owned technology devices

5 Look at the graph in Question 4 again. If the same data set had been collected about a group of teenagers, do you think the graph would look similar? Explain why or why not.

What did you learn?

What should you remember when you read a graph? Why?

148

D Probability

When you roll a dice, the number you get is the **outcome** of that **event**. There are six **possible outcomes** when you roll a normal dice. These outcomes are 1, 2, 3, 4, 5 or 6.

Before you do any **probability experiments** it is useful to think about what outcomes are possible.

Look at this spinner.

What are the possible outcomes when you spin this spinner?

The possible outcomes are red, yellow, green or blue. The arrow could land on any of these colours.

What outcome would you expect? Why?

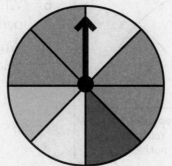

Maths ideas

In this unit you will:
* list the possible outcomes of events
* count and compare the actual outcomes of events.

Key words

outcome	probability
event	experiment
possible outcome	expected outcome

You would probably expect blue, as more sections are blue than any of the other colours.

Remember that an outcome is always one of the possible outcomes, but that it may not be the **expected outcome**. You could spin this spinner a hundred times and it might not land on blue at all. In fact, there is an equal chance of blue or another colour on the spinner because there are four blue sections and four sections with another colour.

1 Look at these spinners.

   a List the possible outcomes for each one.

   b What outcome would you expect if you rolled each one? Why?

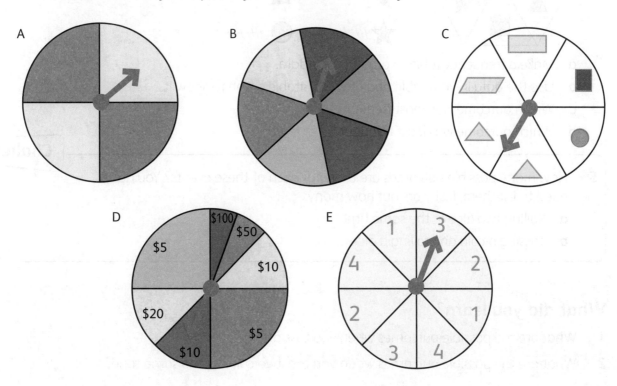

2   Draw and colour a spinner with the following possible outcomes.

   a   Red, black or white

   b   A, B, C or D

   c   A colour or a shape

3   The picture shows a large wheel. It is used in a TV programme called 'Spin and Win'. The contestants on the show spin the wheel to win a prize to which the arrow points.

   a   What are the possible outcomes when you spin the wheel?

   b   Which outcome would you expect most people to get? Why?

   c   Which prize has the lowest probability of being won? Why?

4   Joanne made a spinner like this one. She did 80 spins and tallied the outcomes.

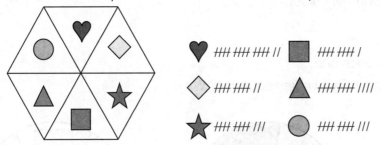

   a   Make a frequency table to organise the data.

   b   Use the data in your table and draw a suitable graph to show it.

   c   Which outcome was most frequent?

   d   Which outcome was least frequent?

Challenge

5   How many possible outcomes are there for each of these events? You don't need to list them, just work out how many.

   a   Rolling two dice at the same time

   b   Tossing a coin and rolling a dice

What did you learn?

1   What are the possible outcomes when you toss a coin?

2   What are the possible outcomes when you toss two coins at the same time?

Topic 15 Review

Key ideas and concepts

Write an email to a classmate who was absent to summarise the main things you learnt in this topic.

Think, talk, write ...

1 Work in pairs. Find three graphs in newspapers or online. Take turns to ask each other questions about the graphs.

2 Which type of graph do you find easiest to read and understand? Why?

Quick check

1 A survey shows the mean time that people spend doing different activities on their mobile phones. Draw a suitable graph to show the data.

Activity	Internet	Social media	Music	Games	Calls	Texts	Email	Photos
Time (in minutes)	25	17	15	14	12.5	10.5	11	4

2 The Fitzgerald family kept track of how much water they used over one week. They collected this set of data.

Monday	Tuesday	Wednesday	Thursday	Friday	Saturday	Sunday
180 ℓ	220 ℓ	150 ℓ	260 ℓ	240 ℓ	120 ℓ	280 ℓ

Draw a suitable graph to show the family's water consumption over the week.

3 These two graphs show how much time two students spent studying each week for a month. Compare the graphs and write notes about what they show.

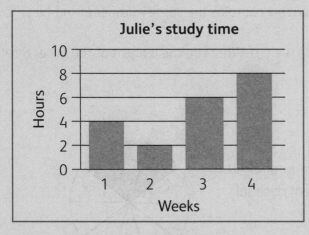

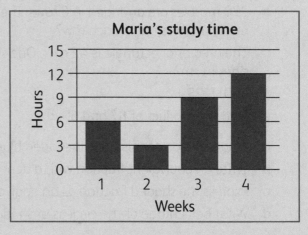

Test yourself 3

Complete this test to check that you have understood and can manage the work covered this year. Revise any sections that you find difficult.

1   a   What is the value of the 5 in the number 753 798?

    b   In which of the numbers below does the place value of the 4 represent ten thousands?

       i   45 368   ii   104 236   iii 765 412

    c   What is the missing number in the sequence 47, 41, 35, _____, 23?

    d   Which prime number is greater than 21 but less than 28?

    e   What is 3 093 rounded to the nearest hundred?

    f   What is the value of the underlined digit in 5.2<u>1</u>?

2   a   What is the difference in value between 461 and 157?

    b   By how much is 6 016 greater than 3 800?

    c   Jerry has some marbles. He received 15 more marbles. He now has 60 marbles. Write a number sentence that best represents this information.

3   a   What is the highest common factor (HCF) of 12, 18 and 24?

    b   Light R flashes every 4 minutes. Light S flashes every 6 minutes. If the two lights flash together at 8:00 a.m., at what time would they flash together again?

4   a   Grenadians pay $0.15 value-added tax (VAT) on each dollar for imported goods. What is the percentage VAT they pay?

    b   270 marbles are arranged in 6 rows. If each row contains the same number of marbles, how many marbles are in each row?

    c   The area of a rectangle is 42 cm². One side is 7 cm. What are the lengths of the other three sides in cm?

    d   500 ÷ 25 = _____

    e   Find the product of 87 and 60.

5   a   What fraction of this circle is shaded blue?

    b   Write an equivalent fraction with a denominator of 40.

    c   Express the shaded fraction as an equivalent decimal.

    d   What percentage of the circle is unshaded?

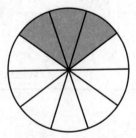

6 Find the difference between $\frac{7}{8}$ and $\frac{3}{4}$.

7 A recipe for making 5 pizzas requires $\frac{3}{4}$ pounds of flour. How many pounds of flour are needed to make 15 pizzas?

8 Arrange the fractions $\frac{1}{2}$, $\frac{5}{6}$ and $\frac{2}{3}$ in ascending order.

9 A pencil is 9 cm long. It is reduced by $\frac{1}{5}$ of its length each time it is sharpened. What will the length be in centimetres, after it is sharpened for the second time?

10 Andrea completed her homework in $1\frac{1}{2}$ hours. Jerry took $2\frac{1}{3}$ hours to do the same homework. How much longer did Jerry take than Rhonda to do the homework?

11 Patrick had a total of $0.95 in coins in his pocket. He bought three 25¢ snacks during recess. How much money does he have left?

12 This table shows the height and mass of three girls who visited a clinic.

Name	Height (m)	Mass (Kg)
Chelsie	1.25	38
Sheena	1.30	41
Myiah	1.48	47

Which of the following statements is true?
a A girl's height is more than her mass.
b The youngest girl has the smallest mass.
c A girl's mass increases as her height increases.

13 a The sum of two numbers is 7.26. If the smaller number is 3.4, what is the larger number?

b Arrange these decimals in ascending order: 5.09; 50.9; 5.90.

c Write the decimal equivalent of $\frac{4}{5}$.

d Find the sum of 7.5, 43.2 and 135.8.

e What is the product of 0.45 and 8?

f What is 2 500 grams expressed as kilograms?

14 Write the time 16:15 using the 12-hour system.

15 What temperature is shown on this thermometer in degrees Celsius?

16 List the name of each angle and say what type of angle it is.

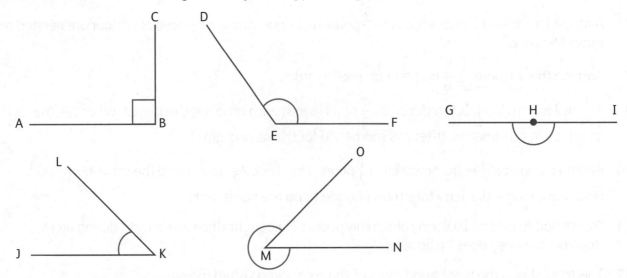

17 a What does the term 'per cent' mean?

    b What percentage of 400 is 40?

    c What is 30 % of $60?

18 A motor cycle travels at an average speed of 30 km per hour. How many minutes will it take to travel 20 km?

19 Devon started a cross-country race at 9:45 a.m. He completed the race at 12:15 p.m. How long did he take to complete the race?

20 a A tourist has these notes in his wallet. How much money is this?

    b Write one thousand and sixty-five dollars and forty-five cents in figures.

21 Chantel has $22.25 and Laura has $41.75.

    a How much more money does Laura have than Chantel?

    b If Chantel gets another $7.75 and Laura gets another $8.25, how much do they each have?

22 Nicole buys this photo frame.

    a What is the perimeter of the frame?

    b What area will the frame take up on her wall?

    c If the frame is 4 cm wide, what is the area of the display window?

20 cm

60 cm

23 Look at these diagrams.

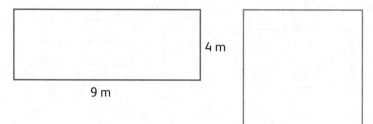

a If the square and the rectangle have the same area, calculate the perimeter of the square in metres.

b What is the area of a rectangle 3 m wide and 5 m long?

24 Look at this diagram of a triangle.

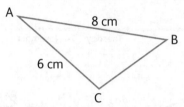

If the perimeter of the triangle is three times the length of AC, calculate the length of BC.

25 How many 250-millilitre bottles can be filled from a container which holds 4 litres?

26 Look at the bar graph shown here.

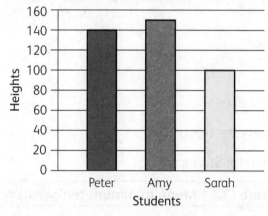

a What interval is used on the vertical axis?

b Suggest a suitable heading for the graph.

c Calculate the mean height of the students.

27 Sarah decided to go for a run. She left her house at quarter past 10 in the morning and returned home at noon.

a What was her starting time in digital notation?

b Write her finishing time in 24-hour format.

c What was the duration of her run?

28 Nick wants to make a small ladder. He needs two longer pieces of wood for the two side rails measuring 1.5 m each. He will have 7 rungs in the ladder measuring 40 cm each. Nick has a 650 cm length of wood.

a Does Nick have enough wood to make his ladder?

b Does he have any wood left over? If so, how much is left over?

29 Which shape represents the net of a cone?

a 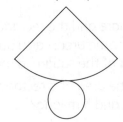   b 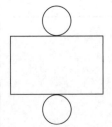   c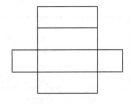

30 Look at this weather meteogram carefully. It shows weather information for Bridgetown in Barbados.

Meteogram, next 48 hours

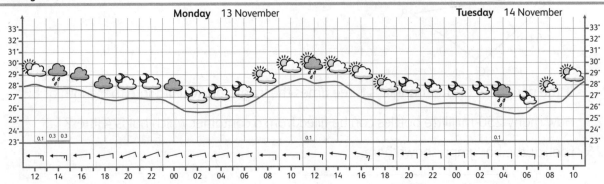

a What types of graph are used to show the data?

b What is shown on the vertical scale?

c What do the blue bars represent?

d How is time shown on the graph?

e What does the graph tell you about the weather over this period?

31 A weather site on the internet gives this information for St Vincent.

Month	Mean maximum temperature (°C)	Mean minimum temperature (°C)
January	28.3	21.4
February	28.4	21.3
March	28.8	21.5
April	29.5	22.2
May	30.1	23.4
June	30.2	24.3
July	30.2	24.3
August	30.5	24.0
September	30.7	23.3
October	30.5	23.0
November	29.9	22.7
December	28.9	21.9

Draw a line graph showing both sets of data on the same set of axes.